Resilient Man:
Conquer Self-Sabotage and Embrace Emotional Vulnerability
2 Books in 1

Master Emotional Intelligence, Build Stronger Relationships, and Achieve Lasting Personal Growth

Richard Garraway

Book 1: Breaking the Cycle of Self-Sabotage for Men

Table of Contents

Book 2: Emotional Vulnerability in Men

Table of Contents

BREAKING THE CYCLE OF *Self—Sabotage* **FOR MEN**

HOW TO OVERCOME OBSTACLES AND ACHIEVE LASTING SUCCESS

RICHARD GARRAWAY

YOUR FREE GIFT

As a special thank you, I'm delighted to offer you a free bonus.
Introducing **"Self-Awareness Assessment Quiz"**
To claim the quiz, please visit:
https://richardgarrawaybooks.com/Free-Gift-4

Why take the quiz?

- **Deep Self-Reflection:** Gain insight into subtle self-sabotaging behaviors.
- **Customized Guidance:** Receive a personalized score and roadmap for change.
- **Empower Personal Growth:** Break free from self-sabotage and pursue success.
- **Control Your Destiny:** Make intentional choices aligning with your goals.

Again, thank you for your support and trust in "Breaking the Cycle of Self-Sabotage"

Richard Garraway

Introduction

Amid the hum of the bustling coffee shop, Mark found himself staring at his laptop screen, his heart racing, his palms damp. It was Monday morning, and he was about to submit the proposal that could potentially change the trajectory of his career. He had poured weeks of effort into crafting the perfect pitch, aligning his ideas with precision, and anticipating every possible question.

As he moved his cursor to click the "Submit" button, a sudden wave of unease swept over him. Doubt crept in as though a shadow had eclipsed the clarity he had just moments ago. "What if it gets rejected?" he thought. "What if I've missed a crucial detail?" An inner voice whispered insidiously, making him hesitate to send the proposal.

Mark began hovering over the mouse with his hands. The seconds felt like an eternity as he grappled with his emotions. He recognized this familiar pattern—his dreams and aspirations clashing head-on with an invisible force, an impulse to undermine his efforts.

Flashbacks of past attempts flooded his mind: the unfinished novel that gathered dust, the gym membership card that barely saw the light of day, the business venture he backed out of at the last minute. Each memory was a testament to a battle he couldn't win—a cycle of potential unmet, dreams unrealized, and self-sabotage perpetuated.

It was in this moment of hesitation that Mark realized he was facing more than just the decision to click a button. He was facing himself—the one who had held him back time and time again, the one who had whispered "not good enough" and "too risky." It was the battle between his yearning for success and the resistance that had become an all-too-familiar companion.

In this single moment, Mark's internal struggle mirrored a universal experience—one that each of us has encountered in our journey toward self-improvement, growth, and achievement. It's the moment when the enormity of our dreams crashes against the wall or our doubts. It's the moment of truth that defines whether we break free from the cycle of self-sabotage or succumb to its grip.

I am not just the author of this book; I am also on this journey with you. I've wrestled with self-doubt, stared down the abyss of missed opportunities, and emerged stronger, wiser, and more determined to share the insights I've gathered. Through research, personal experience, and a deep passion for empowering others, I've been able to overcome the challenges of self-doubt, and I understand your struggles and believe unequivocally in your ability to overcome them. I understand the pain of setting goals only to find that they remain tantalizingly out of reach.

The frustration of starting strong only to sabotage progress when the finish line draws near. The quiet desperation of witnessing others achieve what you long for, wondering why it seems so elusive for you.

As we journey through the pages ahead, remember that the recognition of your struggles is not an indictment of your worthiness. It's an affirmation that your experiences are valid, your pain is acknowledged, and your capacity for transformation is immense. You're not defined by the moments of self-sabotage; you're defined by your courage to confront them.

For those who have experienced the sinking sensation of watching dreams slip through their fingers, this book is a testament to your journey. This book is a mirror that reflects your challenges, a lantern that illuminates your path, and a bridge that connects you with the strategies and insights to overcome the forces that have held you back. Let's embark on this shared expedition toward a life liberated from the clutches of self-sabotage.

In the pages of this book, you're not just encountering a collection of words; you're embarking on a transformative journey that holds the key to unlocking your fullest potential. This book is a compass guiding you through the uncharted territories of your mind, helping you break free from the shackles of self-doubt and embrace the boundless possibilities that await.

Each chapter is a stepping stone, and each exercise is a tool to equip you with the skills necessary to break free from the grip of self-sabotage and step into the fullness of your potential.

On this journey of self-improvement, the pursuit of our highest potential is both exhilarating and challenging. It's a road paved with aspirations, dreams, and the promise of a better life. "Breaking the Cycle of Self-Sabotage for Men" is not just a book; it's a compass that will guide you through the labyrinth of self-doubt, hesitation, and self-sabotage. By embarking on this transformative journey, you're opening the door to a wealth of benefits that will ripple through every facet of your life.

1. Self-Awareness and Understanding. Gain a profound understanding of why you sabotage your success and how past experiences have shaped your current patterns.

2. Strategies for Lasting Change. This book isn't just about temporary fixes; it's about equipping you with practical strategies that create lasting change. Discover proven techniques to challenge negative self-talk, overcome fear, and cultivate a resilient mindset.

3. Empowerment and Confidence. As you unravel the layers of self-sabotage, you'll uncover the wellspring of your true potential. You will no longer be held back by self-imposed limitations; instead, you will stand tall in your pursuits.

4. Goal Achievement. With the insights and techniques in this book, you'll no longer sabotage your progress when success is on the horizon. Instead, you'll be equipped to overcome obstacles, push through setbacks, and celebrate achievements without hesitation.

5. Enhanced Relationships. Self-sabotage not only affects personal goals but can also impact relationships. By breaking the cycle, you'll build healthier connections based on authenticity and self-assurance.

6. Lifelong Transformation. The journey outlined in this book is not a fleeting moment; it's a life-altering expedition. As you internalize the lessons and practices, you'll create a foundation for ongoing growth, resilience, and fulfillment.

Every page of this book is a step closer to your true potential. The benefits extend far beyond the confines of the book, seeping into your thoughts, actions, and the life you lead. By investing in this journey, you're investing in yourself—a decision that has the power to reshape your future and ignite a transformation that reverberates for years to come.

By turning these pages, you're embarking on a profound voyage—a voyage that will reshape your perceptions, ignite your passions, and empower you to transcend self-sabotage. The benefits of reading this book are not just confined to its content; they extend to every facet of your life that is waiting to be enriched, elevated, and transformed.

From there, you'll be guided through transformative strategies that will empower you to break free from self-imposed limitations and reclaim control over your destiny.

This book stands as a beacon of guidance and empowerment. As you read this book, it will help you with:

1. Understanding Self-Sabotage. Explore the deep-rooted causes and triggers of self-sabotage, unraveling its psychological underpinnings to gain a clear grasp of why it occurs.

2. Confronting Negative Self-Talk. Learn to identify and challenge the destructive inner dialogues that foster self-sabotage, replacing them with affirming thoughts that cultivate self-confidence.

3. Harnessing Fear and Resistance. Embrace fear as a transformative force, understand how to leverage it to your advantage, and navigate resistance in pursuit of your goals.

4. Nurturing Self-Compassion. Cultivate self-compassion as a shield against self-sabotage, foster a kinder relationship with yourself, and nurture your growth.

5. Strategic Goal Setting. Develop effective goal-setting strategies that align with your values, accompanied by actionable plans to ensure steady progress and minimize self-sabotage risks.

6. Bouncing Back from Setbacks. Equip yourself with resilience tools to recover from setbacks and failures, learning to see them as integral steps on the path to success.

7. Cultivating a Growth Mindset. Embrace a growth mindset that views challenges as opportunities for growth, enabling you to navigate uncertainties and failures with tenacity.

8. Building Empowering Habits. Create routines and habits that counteract self-sabotaging tendencies by reinforcing positive behavior patterns and cultivating consistency.

9. Nurturing Authentic Relationships. Develop relationships that support your growth and well-being, learning how to establish boundaries and communicate effectively to prevent self-sabotage triggers.

10. Sustaining Lasting Change. Craft a personalized plan for continued self-empowerment, ensuring that the knowledge and strategies gained from the book become an enduring part of your journey.

These lessons collectively empower you to break the cycle of self-sabotage, replace limiting beliefs with empowering ones, and take charge of your life's trajectory. By embracing these strategies, you'll embark on a transformative journey toward purpose, fulfillment, and unrestrained achievement.

I have a commitment to helping individuals overcome self-sabotage that stems from both personal experience and a dedicated pursuit of expertise. I've faced the battles of doubt, hesitation, and self-imposed limitations, and I've emerged stronger, wiser, and more resolute in my mission to share the insights I've gained. This book isn't just a collection of theories; it's a culmination of my own journey and my passion for helping others find their way.

As a communication expert, I've dedicated years to understanding the complexities of human behavior, personal development, and the psychology behind self-sabotage. My commitment to ongoing research and learning ensures that the strategies within this book are not only rooted in proven methods but also tailored to the unique challenges faced by men striving for personal growth and success.

As you hold this book in your hands, you've taken a crucial step toward transforming your life. The fact that you're reading this, seeking answers and solutions, is a testament to your readiness for change. The journey ahead isn't about quick fixes or empty promises; it's about real, sustainable transformation.

This is the book for you if you are tired of being held back by your own doubts and fears. It's for the ones who are tired of watching their potential go unrealized, those who are yearning for a life defined by authenticity, accomplishment, and fulfillment.

Through real-life events, evidence-based strategies, and actionable steps, this book is tailored to resonate with your experiences and aspirations. It's designed to empower you with the tools to break free from the self-sabotaging cycle, forge an unshakable mindset, and confidently stride toward the life you envision. I'm committed to helping people break free of self-sabotaging and find real direction in their lives.

Remember, this isn't just a book; it's a roadmap to your own transformation—a journey that's both deeply personal and universally relatable. By investing in yourself through these pages, you're signaling to the universe—and to yourself—that you're ready to rise above the constraints of self-sabotage and claim the success and happiness you deserve.

As you embark on this odyssey through the realms of self-discovery and transformation, remember this: you possess an innate power and a strength that can withstand the onslaught of self-sabotage. The journey won't be without its challenges, but with each page turned, you'll move closer to the life you've envisioned—one free from self-imposed limitations, one fueled by your untamed potential.

In the pages that follow, we'll unravel the mysteries of self-sabotage, diving deep into its causes and effects. You will be equipped with the tools, strategies, and insights you need to conquer the relentless cycles that have held you back. But before we embark on this journey, let's explore the enigma of self-sabotage itself—how it manifests, why it takes root and the profound impact it can have on our lives.

Get ready to rebuild the walls of your ambitions, challenge the doubts that have muted your potential, and step boldly into a future defined not by self-sabotage but by purpose, achievement, and the unyielding belief in your own worthiness. Let's get started and explore the path to your true potential!

Part 1: Understanding the Cycle of Self-Sabotage

Chapter 1: Identifying Your Self-Sabotaging Behaviors

Have you ever felt like you were taking one step forward and two steps back? You set goals and make plans, and yet somehow, you find yourself repeatedly stumbling into obstacles that hinder your progress. This frustrating cycle is often the result of something deeply ingrained within us: self-sabotage.

Self-sabotage is the dark side of ambition. It is the part of us that is afraid of success and will do anything to keep us from achieving our goals. Self-sabotage is the voice in our heads that tells us we're not good enough. It is the fear of failure that holds us back from taking risks and living our best lives. Self-sabotage is the comfort zone we refuse to leave. It is the familiar pain we choose over the possibility of something better.

Imagine when a new opportunity comes, giving you a chance to step into your potential, and your heart bursts out with excitement. Your heart races with excitement as you imagine the possibilities that lie ahead. You've crafted a plan, visualized success, and even taken the first few steps. But as you proceed, an invisible force seems to pull you back. Doubt creeps in like a shadow, and then you begin to second-guess yourself, thinking that you're not good enough and that failure is inevitable. It's as though there's a hidden hand working against your efforts, derailing your progress, and sabotaging your success. You're left baffled and frustrated, wondering why your own actions seem to be your greatest obstacle. This is the intricate art of self-sabotage, which countless individuals engage in without even realizing it.

In this chapter, we'll delve into the concept of self-sabotage, unveiling its cunning disguises and shedding light on how to break free from its grip and live a life of authenticity and freedom. From procrastination that stirs up laziness to the paralyzing grip of perfectionism, we'll demystify the pattern by which self-sabotage can keep you from reaching your full potential. It's time to unravel the puzzle, decode the patterns, and equip yourself with the tools to conquer self-sabotage and move forward with unwavering confidence. Are you ready to take the first step toward liberation from the cycle of self-sabotage?

Recognizing Self-Sabotage

Have you ever put off doing something important even though you knew you should? Maybe you had a big test coming up, but you couldn't bring yourself to start studying. Or maybe you had a job interview, but you kept putting off practicing your answers, even when that tiny voice kept telling you to do what you were supposed to do, but you couldn't bring yourself to do it. If so, you're not alone. Procrastination is a common problem that affects people of all ages and backgrounds.

Procrastination as a Form of Self-Sabotage

Procrastination is often seen as a harmless habit, but it can actually be a form of self-sabotage. When we procrastinate, we are essentially sabotaging our own goals and dreams. We are telling ourselves that we are not good enough or that we are not capable of success.

There are many reasons why people procrastinate. Some people procrastinate because they are afraid of failure. Others procrastinate because they are perfectionists and want to do everything perfectly. And still, others procrastinate because they lack self-belief and don't believe in themselves.

Procrastination only provides you with temporary relief from the discomfort of tackling a challenging task, but beneath its deceptive comfort lies a feeling of inadequacy and failure.

Intentional Delay or Self-Sabotaging Procrastination?

The difference between intentional delay and Self-sabotaging Procrastination lies between intention and outcome. Not all procrastination is self-sabotaging. Sometimes, we procrastinate because we are simply busy or because we have other priorities. This is called intentional delay. Intentional delay is a normal part of life and is not harmful.

Self-sabotaging procrastination, on the other hand, is when we procrastinate for negative reasons. We may procrastinate because we are afraid of failure or because we are scared that we are not good enough to succeed at something. Self-sabotaging procrastination can be very harmful because it can prevent us from achieving our goals and living our best lives.

The Role of Fear, Perfectionism, and Lack of Self-Belief in Procrastination

Fear, perfectionism, and a lack of self-belief are all common factors that contribute to procrastination. When we are afraid of failure, we may procrastinate as a way to avoid the possibility of disappointment. Perfectionists may procrastinate because they are afraid of making mistakes. And people with low self-belief may procrastinate because they don't believe they are capable of success.

If you are struggling with procrastination, it is important to understand the reasons why you are doing it. Once you understand the underlying causes, you can start to develop strategies for overcoming procrastination.

Breaking Free: A Practical Approach

Recognizing self-sabotaging procrastination is the first step toward liberation. The next step is understanding why you are always trapped in it and then breaking down the barriers that fuel this behavior. Start by acknowledging your fears, whether they're related to failure, success, or a particular aspect of the task. Bringing these fears to light reduces their power over your actions.

Challenge your perfectionist behavior by setting realistic goals for yourself. Accept that imperfection is a natural part of growth and learning. Break down tasks into smaller, manageable steps, allowing you to make progress without feeling overwhelmed by the pursuit of perfection.

Boosting self-belief requires conscious effort. Create a list of your accomplishments, skills, and strengths. Reflect on past achievements to remind yourself of your capabilities. Building self-belief takes time, but with consistent practice, you'll find yourself more inclined to take action.

Self-Doubt and Negative Self-Talk

Self-doubt and negative self-talk are two of the most common forms of self-sabotage. They can have a destructive impact on our endeavors, making it difficult to achieve our goals and live the lives we want.

Self-doubt is a seemingly harmless feeling that holds within itself the power to shape our reality. It's like a tiny voice that whispers at the back of your mind, bringing in a feeling of uncertainty with every step you take. This self-doubt is the critical, judgmental, and pessimistic inner dialogue we have with ourselves, which is fostered by negative self-talk. It can be about our appearance, our abilities, our worth, or anything else about ourselves. Negative self-talk can have a negative impact on our thoughts, feelings, and behaviors and can make it difficult to achieve our goals and live our best lives.

The Destructive Impact of Self-Doubt

Self-doubt operates like an undercurrent; it convinces us that we're ill-equipped, unworthy, or bound to fail. As a result, we might hesitate to seize opportunities, opt for safer choices, or abandon pursuits altogether. Recognizing the nature of self-doubt is the first step in breaking free from its hold.

Self-doubt is the belief that we are not good enough or capable enough to succeed. It can manifest in a variety of ways, such as:

1. Procrastination. We put off starting or finishing tasks because we don't think we can do them well.

2. Perfectionism. We set unrealistic standards for ourselves and then beat ourselves up when we don't meet them.

3. Fear of failure. We avoid taking risks or trying new things because we're afraid of failing.

4. Low Self-Esteem. We have a negative view of ourselves and our abilities.

Self-doubt can be a very powerful force, holding us back from achieving our goals and living our best lives. It can be difficult to overcome, but it is possible with time and effort.

Identifying the Subtle Ways Negative Self-Talk Reinforces Self-Sabotage

Negative self-talk is often so subtle that we hardly notice it's there. It creeps in as self-awareness or realism, tricking us into believing its validity. "I'm just being practical," you might tell yourself, not realizing that these seemingly pragmatic thoughts are actually fueling the cycle of self-doubt and self-sabotage.

Have you ever noticed that whenever we tend to doubt our ability to do something, we tend to fail at it? If you tell yourself that you're not good enough, you're less likely to try new things or take risks. If you tell yourself that you're going to fail, you're more likely to give up when things get tough. And if you tell yourself that you don't deserve success, you will find it hard to celebrate your achievements.

Strategies to Recognize and Reframe Negative Thought Patterns

1. Pay Attention to Your Thoughts. The first step is to become aware of your thoughts. When you notice a negative thought, ask yourself where it came from and what purpose it serves.

2. Challenge Your Thoughts. Once you're aware of your negative thoughts, challenge them. Ask yourself if they're really true or if they're just based on fear or past experiences.

3. Replace Negative Thoughts with Positive Ones. Once you've challenged your negative thoughts, replace them with positive ones. This can be difficult at first, but it gets easier with practice.

4. Focus on Your Strengths. Instead of focusing on your weaknesses, focus on your strengths. What are you good at? What are you proud of?

5. Be Kind to Yourself. Talk to yourself the way you would talk to a friend. Be patient and understanding, and don't give up on yourself.

Overcoming self-doubt and negative self-talk is a journey, not a destination. It takes time and effort, but it is possible.

The Deceptive Comfort Zone

Our comfort zone is the psychological state in which we operate our familiar routines and experiences, where there is minimal stress and risk. It is a space where a person feels at ease, confident, and in control, typically engaging in activities or situations that are well-known and require minimal effort. Remaining within one's comfort zone provides a sense of security and predictability, but it often limits personal growth, learning, and the pursuit of new challenges. Stepping out of the comfort zone involves venturing into unfamiliar territory, where there may be uncertainty, anxiety, and a need to adapt. This deliberate act of pushing beyond familiar boundaries is a crucial aspect of personal development, enabling individuals to acquire new skills, broaden their experiences, and realize their full potential.

How Staying Within Your Comfort Zone Can Lead to Self-Sabotage

When we stay within our comfort zones, we're not challenging ourselves or growing. We're not learning new things or taking on new challenges. And this can lead to feelings of boredom, stagnation, and dissatisfaction.

Staying within your comfort zone can make you more susceptible to self-sabotage. This is because you're not used to taking risks or stepping outside of your comfort zone. So when you do try something new, you may be more likely to give up easily or sabotage your own success.

Consider this: staying within your comfort zone might mean avoiding challenges or risks, limiting your exposure to new experiences, and suppressing growth opportunities. Over time, this avoidance not only hinders your progress but unknowingly fuels self-sabotage.

Strategies to Gradually Expand Your Comfort Zone

The good news is that breaking free from the comfort zone's grasp is what you are capable of doing. Here are some strategies that can help you gradually expand your comfort zone and embrace growth:

1. Set Small Goals. Begin with small steps outside your comfort zone. These small goals can be as simple as initiating a conversation with a new colleague or trying a new type of cuisine. Gradually, as you accomplish these minor victories, your comfort zone will expand.

2. Take Baby Steps. When you're trying something new, don't expect it to be perfect right away. Just take baby steps and gradually increase your comfort level. Challenge yourself to engage in activities that make you uneasy, one step at a time, whether it's public speaking, joining a social gathering, or taking up a new hobby. As you face these situations, your confidence will grow, and so will your comfort zone.

3. Practice Mindfulness. Mindfulness is a powerful tool for self-discovery and growth. Engage in activities mindfully, paying attention to your thoughts and emotions. This practice can help you identify moments when you're resisting change and provide the opportunity to question those reactions.

4. Seek Support and Accountability. Get an accountability partner; it may be friends, mentors, or coaches who can encourage you to step outside your comfort zone. Having someone to share your journey with can provide motivation and accountability.

5. Celebrate Every Step. Acknowledge and celebrate your progress, no matter how small. Each time you reach a stage beyond your comfort zone, you appreciate yourself for doing so. By recognizing these achievements, you reinforce the positive changes you're making.

As you stretch out of your comfort zone, you'll notice a gradual shift—that which once caused discomfort becomes the norm. This change not only weakens the grip of self-sabotage but also opens doors to new opportunities and personal growth.

Fear of Success and Failure

Many people are afraid of success. They worry about what it will mean for their career, their identity, their relationships, or their sense of security. They may also be afraid of the expectations that come with success.

Others are afraid of failure. They worry about what it will mean for their self-esteem, their confidence, or their ability to achieve their goals. They may also be afraid of what others think of them.

But what many people don't realize is that it's possible to be afraid of both success and failure. This paradoxical fear can be very debilitating, as it can prevent us from taking risks and pursuing our goals.

How These Fears Manifest

You'd think these two concepts would stand on opposite ends of the emotional spectrum, but no, they sometimes intertwine and create a storm of contradictory emotions within us.

The fear of success can manifest in these ways, including:

- Procrastination: We put off taking action because we're afraid of what might happen if we succeed.

- Perfectionism: We set unrealistic standards for ourselves and then beat ourselves up when we don't meet them.

- Self-sabotage: We sabotage our own success by making excuses, giving up easily, or taking unnecessary risks.

The fear of failure can manifest in these ways, including:

- Avoiding challenges: We avoid taking on new challenges because we're afraid of failing.

- Avoiding risk: We choose the safe option, even if it's not the best option, because we're afraid of taking risks.

- Self-doubt: We doubt our abilities and give up easily because we're afraid of failing.

Embracing a Balanced Perspective on Success and Failure

The first step to overcoming the fear of success and failure is to understand that both are part of life. Everyone experiences both success and failure at some point. It's how we respond to these experiences that matter.

If we can learn to understand the perspective of success and failure, we can overcome our fear of both. This means accepting that failure is a natural part of the learning process and that it doesn't mean we're failures. It also means celebrating our successes, no matter how small.

Here are some tips for embracing a balanced perspective on success and failure:

1. Reframe Your Thinking About Success and Failure. Instead of seeing success as the opposite of failure, see them as two sides of the same coin. Both are necessary for growth and learning.

2. Focus on the Process, Not the Outcome. When you concentrate on the process of achieving your goals, you are less likely to be discouraged by setbacks.

3. Celebrate Your Successes, No Matter How Small. When you take the time to celebrate your successes, you'll start to see yourself as a capable and successful person.

4. Be Kind to Yourself. Everyone Makes Mistakes. When you make a mistake, don't beat yourself up about it. Learn from your mistakes and move on.

Overcoming the fear of success and failure is a journey, not a destination. It takes time and effort, but it is possible.

Perfectionism Paralysis

Perfectionism is the tendency to set unrealistic standards and be overly critical of our own performance. It can be a very debilitating trait, as it can prevent us from taking risks, facing challenges, trying new things, and achieving our goals.

When perfectionism becomes extreme, it can lead to perfectionism paralysis. Perfectionism paralysis is the inability to take action because we're afraid of not being perfect. We may procrastinate, overthink, or give up easily because we're afraid of making mistakes.

Understanding the Connection Between Perfectionism and Self-Sabotage

Perfectionism and self-sabotage are closely related. Perfectionism can lead to self-sabotage in the following ways:

- **Procrastination.** We may procrastinate because we're afraid of not being perfect. We may think that if we wait until we're perfect, then we'll be able to do the task perfectly. But the problem is that we never feel perfect, so we never take action.

- **Overthinking.** We may overthink a task because we're afraid of making a mistake. We may worry about every little detail and second-guess ourselves. This can lead to paralysis, as we're unable to make a decision or take action.

- **Giving Up Easily.** We may give up easily because we're afraid of not being perfect. We may think that if we don't get it right the first time, then it's not worth trying. This can prevent us from achieving our goals.

Recognizing the Signs of Perfectionism-Driven Inaction

Perfectionism-driven inaction is a term used to describe the inability to take action because of a fear of not being perfect. This can manifest in a variety of ways, such as procrastination, overthinking, and giving up easily. Perfectionism-driven inaction can be a very weakening trait, as it can prevent us from achieving our goals and living our best lives.

Perfectionism-driven inaction operates in disguise. On the surface, you may appear to be striving for the best, giving your all to achieve your goals, but on the inside, you are trapped by the belief that anything less than perfection is unacceptable. As a result, you might find yourself stuck in a cycle of never truly completing or beginning what you were meant to do. The fear of imperfection can paralyze you, leading you to delay taking action until every detail aligns with your ideal. This self-imposed standard not only hinders your progress but also robs you of celebrating success.

If you're struggling with perfectionism paralysis, there are a few signs to look out for:

1. You procrastinate on tasks.

2. You overthink decisions.

3. You give up easily.

4. You're afraid of making mistakes.

5. You're constantly comparing yourself to others.

6. You're never satisfied with your own work.

Cultivating a Healthy Struggle for Excellence Without Succumbing to Self-Sabotage

Striving for excellence is an admirable pursuit that can drive you to achieve remarkable feats. It's essential to recognize that perfection is an unattainable goal; it's a mirage that keeps moving farther away as you approach it. Instead, focus on your journey and the incremental steps you're taking toward improvement.

Consider reframing your mindset from "perfection" to "excellence." Excellence acknowledges the beauty of imperfection and places value on the process as much as the outcome. Break down your goals into manageable tasks, and celebrate each milestone you achieve. Remember that setbacks are not failures; they're opportunities to learn and refine your approach. Embrace the idea that your value isn't tied to flawless results but rather to your dedication, effort, and resilience.

Scientific research underscores the detriments of extreme perfectionism. Studies have linked perfectionism to increased stress, anxiety, and depression, while moderate striving for excellence is associated with higher achievement and greater life satisfaction. By acknowledging the imperfections within ourselves and our endeavors, we can alleviate the pressure that breeds self-sabotage.

If you're struggling with perfectionism paralysis, there are a few steps you can take to overcome it:

1. Redefine Perfection. Perfection is an unattainable goal. Instead, focus on striving for excellence. Excellence means doing your best and giving it your all. It doesn't mean being perfect.

2. Accept Imperfection. Everyone makes mistakes. It's part of being human. Learn to accept your own imperfections and learn from your mistakes.

4. Focus on the Process, Not the Outcome. Don't get so caught up in the outcome of a task that you forget to enjoy the process. Focus on doing your best and learning along the way.

5. Be Kind to Yourself. Don't be so hard on yourself when you make mistakes. Everyone makes mistakes. Forgive yourself and move on.

6. Seek Professional Help. If you're struggling to overcome perfectionist paralysis on your own, consider seeking professional help. A therapist can help you understand your perfectionism and develop strategies for overcoming it.

Key Takeaways

- Self-doubt and negative self-talk can lead to procrastination, perfectionism, and fear of failure.

- Staying within our comfort zone can lead to boredom, stagnation, and dissatisfaction.

- The fear of success and failure can lead to procrastination, perfectionism, and self-sabotage.

- Perfectionism can lead to procrastination, overthinking, and giving up easily.

- Perfection is an unattainable goal. Instead, focus on striving for excellence.

- Accept imperfection. Everyone makes mistakes. It's part of being human.

- Focus on the process, not the outcome.

- Be kind to yourself. Don't be so hard on yourself when you make mistakes.

- Seek professional help if you're struggling to overcome self-sabotage on your own.

- Self-sabotage is a journey, not a destination. It takes time and effort, but it is possible to overcome it.

Now that you've gained insight into the web of self-sabotage, it's time to take deliberate action. Reflect on your own experiences, recognizing moments when self-sabotage has held you back. Begin by selecting one self-sabotaging behavior you'd like to address and applying the strategies discussed in this chapter. Break the cycle by taking a proactive step toward your goal and observing the transformative impact it has on your journey.

In the upcoming chapter, we'll delve into the art of understanding self-sabotage and its root causes. By unraveling the psychological factors that fuel these behaviors, you'll be equipped with invaluable insights to reclaim control over your actions and set the stage for profound personal growth. Don't miss this opportunity to unlock your potential and gain clarity in your career direction.

Chapter 2: Understanding the Root Causes of Self-Sabotage

Have you ever felt as if your actions were being guided by an unseen force? You set out with determination, ready to conquer your challenges, yet somehow, you find yourself veering off course, sabotaging your own progress.

Imagine you've been invited to be the keynote speaker at a conference. Despite being an eloquent public speaker accustomed to addressing sizable audiences with expertise, a sense of unease washes over you. Doubts creep in, questioning your ability to deliver effectively.

In this chapter, we'll study the root causes of self-sabotage, unraveling the layers to discover its roots. Just as the forest harbors ancient trees that hold secrets, so do our minds house the beliefs and experiences that shape our actions.

Imagine a tree with gnarled roots extending deep into the ground. To truly comprehend its nature and influence, one must excavate beneath the surface. Similarly, the roots of self-sabotage go deep into our subconscious, shaped by experiences, beliefs, and fears that often stem from our past. Recognizing these roots is not only an act of self-awareness, but it is also a crucial step towards reclaiming control over our actions.

As we delve into the tangled undergrowth of the mind, you'll discover how childhood imprints, limiting beliefs, fear's iron grip, the influence of past failures, and the allure of external validation constitute the intricate tapestry of self-sabotage. This chapter serves as a guide to take you through the labyrinthine passages of your psyche and shed light on the forces that have conspired to hold you back.

In the pursuit of personal evolution, understanding the root causes of self-sabotage is akin to deciphering a map to empowerment. It's a journey that requires introspection, courage, and an unwavering commitment to growth.

This chapter marks a pivotal juncture in your journey to disengage from the cycle of self-sabotage. By the end of this chapter, you'll not only possess a profound understanding of the origins of self-sabotage but also learn strategies to forge a path toward liberation.

Impact of Childhood Experiences

Do you ever wonder why certain challenges trigger self-sabotage in your adult life? The beliefs and attitudes we develop in childhood can shape our self-esteem, our expectations for ourselves, and our reactions to failure. Our early years shape the lens through which we perceive the world, influencing our beliefs, behaviors, and reactions. This chapter is going to shed light on the profound impact of childhood experiences on adult self-sabotage, unveiling how the beliefs and patterns formed during those formative years continue to echo through our lives.

The Blueprint of Beliefs

Imagine your childhood as the blueprint for the person you've become. During this tender age, your mind is remarkably receptive, absorbing information like a sponge. As you interact with your family, peers, and environment, you form beliefs about your worthiness, success, and failure. These beliefs, often ingrained at a subconscious level, lay the foundation for your self-concept and actions in adulthood.

Research in developmental psychology suggests that our early interactions with our environment play a pivotal role in shaping our self-esteem and emotional well-being. Children who receive consistent love, support, and encouragement tend to develop a more positive self-image and a belief in their abilities. On the other hand, children subjected to criticism, neglect, or unrealistic expectations may internalize feelings of inadequacy or develop a fear of failure.

If we received negative messages about ourselves in childhood, such as "You're not good enough" or "You'll never amount to anything," we may carry these messages with us into adulthood, and it can lead to low self-esteem and a belief that we're not capable of achieving our goals.

Ultimately, if we experienced trauma in childhood due to abuse, neglect, or abandonment, we may be more likely to self-sabotage as adults. This is because trauma can damage our sense of self and our ability to trust others. It can also lead to difficulty coping with stress and difficult emotions.

Uncovering How Early Beliefs About Worthiness, Success, and Failure Can Shape Behavior

The beliefs we develop in childhood about worthiness, success, and failure can have a profound impact on our adult self-sabotage. If we believe that we're not worthy of love or success, we may be more likely to sabotage our own chances of achieving our goals. We may also be more likely to set unrealistic expectations for ourselves, which can lead to disappointment and self-doubt.

Recognizing Patterns of the Past

Understanding the impact of childhood experiences on adult self-sabotage begins with recognizing the patterns. Take a moment to reflect on your own upbringing. What messages did you receive about success, failure, and your worthiness? Were you encouraged to take risks and learn from mistakes, or were you met with criticism and unrealistic expectations?

These reflections can reveal the roots of self-sabotaging behaviors. If you find yourself procrastinating on important tasks, fearing failure, or doubting your worthiness, it's possible that these patterns trace back to your early years.

Tips for Overcoming the Impact of Childhood Experiences on Self-Sabotage

If you're struggling to overcome the impact of childhood experiences on your self-sabotage, here are a few tips:

1. Seek Therapy. If you've experienced trauma or neglect in childhood, therapy can be a helpful way to heal and develop healthier coping mechanisms.

2. Do Your Own Inner Work. There are many books and resources available that can help you explore your childhood experiences and develop a deeper understanding of yourself.

3. Challenge Your Negative Beliefs. Pay attention to the negative beliefs you have about yourself and your abilities. Challenge these beliefs with evidence to the contrary.

4. Set Realistic Expectations. Don't set yourself up for failure by setting unrealistic expectations for yourself. Break down your goals into smaller, more manageable steps.

5. Be Patient and Kind to Yourself. It takes time and effort to overcome the impact of childhood experiences. Be patient with yourself, and don't give up.

The Power of Limiting Beliefs

Do you sometimes second-guess yourself when you're on the brink of success, thinking that you don't have the capability to succeed at something? Perhaps you've questioned your own worthiness, thinking, "Do I really deserve this?" These self-doubting thoughts are frequently triggered by limiting beliefs.

Limiting beliefs are the thoughts and beliefs we have about ourselves and our capabilities that hold us back from achieving our goals. They are frequently influenced by our previous experiences, but they can also be influenced by our environment, upbringing, and relationships.

How Limiting Beliefs Become the Driving Force Behind Self-Sabotage

Limiting beliefs can become the driving force behind self-sabotage in various ways. For instance, if we believe that we're not good enough, we may avoid taking risks or trying new things. We may also procrastinate or sabotage our own efforts because we're afraid of failing.

Common Limiting Beliefs

Have you ever been presented with an exciting job opportunity that aligns perfectly with your skills and interests, yet the moment you contemplate applying, that insidious belief surfaces, taunting you with questions like, "Why would they hire me?" or "What if I can't handle it?" These questions are the offspring of limiting beliefs, and if left unchallenged, they can deter you from seizing the opportunity.

Some common limiting beliefs include:

1. I'm not good enough. This is one of the most common limiting beliefs. It can lead to self-doubt, procrastination, and giving up easily.

2. I don't deserve success. This belief can prevent us from taking risks or going after our goals. We may feel like we don't deserve to be happy or successful.

3. I'm not capable of change. This belief can prevent us from trying new things or stepping outside of our comfort zone.

4. I'm not worthy of love. This belief can lead to low self-esteem and difficulty forming healthy relationships.

5. The world is against me. This belief can lead to a victim mentality and make it difficult to take responsibility for our own lives.

Challenging and Reframing Limiting Beliefs

The power to break free from the grip of limiting beliefs lies in your ability to challenge and reframe them. This process involves a shift in perspective—a conscious effort to replace self-doubt with self-belief.

Start by becoming aware of these beliefs when they arise. Pay attention to the moments when you hear that inner critic whispering doubt in your ear. Once identified, ask yourself, "Is this belief based on facts or my perception?" Often, you'll find that these beliefs are unfounded, born from past experiences that no longer hold relevance.

Overcoming limiting beliefs takes time and effort. It's important to be patient with ourselves and not give up. We can also seek professional help if we need it. With time and effort, we can break free from the grip of limiting beliefs and achieve our goals.

Here are a few tips for overcoming limiting beliefs:

1. Become Aware of Your Beliefs. The first step to overcoming limiting beliefs is to become aware of them. Pay attention to the thoughts that go through your head and identify the negative ones.

2. Challenge Your Beliefs. Once you're aware of your limiting beliefs, start challenging them. Ask yourself if there is any evidence to support these beliefs. Are they really true?

3. Reframe Your Beliefs. Once you've challenged your beliefs, try to reframe them in a more positive light. For example, if you believe that you're not good enough, try to reframe that belief as "I'm always learning and growing."

4. Take Action. The best way to overcome limiting beliefs is to take action. Start by setting small, achievable goals for yourself. As you achieve these goals, you'll start to build confidence, and your limiting beliefs will start to lose their power.

5. Be Patient and Kind to Yourself. It takes time and effort to overcome limiting beliefs. Don't expect things to change overnight. Be patient with yourself and be kind to yourself.

The Role of Fear and Trauma

Fear and trauma can play a significant role in self-sabotage. When we experience fear or trauma, our brains go into survival mode. Traumatic experiences can leave deep scars on our minds, instilling beliefs that we are not safe, not worthy, or destined to fail. This can lead to a number of self-sabotaging behaviors, such as avoidance, procrastination, and self-destructive behavior.

How Unresolved Past Traumas Can Manifest as Self-Sabotaging Behaviors

Unresolved past traumas can also manifest as self-sabotaging behaviors. This is because when we don't deal with our past traumas, they can continue to affect us in the present. For example, if we experience abuse or neglect in childhood, we may be more likely to sabotage our relationships or our careers as adults.

Strategies for Healing from Past Traumas to Disrupt the Cycle of Self-Sabotage

There are a number of strategies that can help us heal from past traumas and disrupt the cycle of self-sabotage. These include:

1. Talk Therapy. Therapy can help us understand our past traumas and how they are affecting us in the present.

2. Mindfulness. Mindfulness practices can help us become more aware of our thoughts and feelings and learn to cope with them in a healthy way.

3. Journaling. Writing about your experiences and emotions can be a powerful way to process trauma. It allows you to externalize your feelings, gain insights, and track your healing progress.

4. Support Network. Lean on your support network of friends and loved ones. Sharing your experiences can be cathartic, and their understanding and empathy can be instrumental in your healing process.

5. Self-Care. Taking care of ourselves physically and emotionally can help us feel stronger and more resilient.

The Influence of Past Failures

Past failures can have a significant impact on our self-esteem and our ability to achieve our goals. When we fail, it can be easy to get discouraged and give up. We may start to believe that we're not good enough or that we'll never succeed. This can lead to self-sabotage, such as procrastination, perfectionism, and negative self-talk.

How Past Failures Can Become Anchors of Self-Sabotage

When we fail, it can be tempting to dwell on our mistakes. We may replay the event over and over in our minds, focusing on everything we did wrong. This can lead to negative self-talk and a belief that we're not capable of success. This can become an anchor that weighs us down and prevents us from moving forward.

How the Fear of Repeating Failures Can Hinder Progress

The fear of repeating past failures can also be a major obstacle to success. When we're afraid of failing, we may avoid taking risks or trying new things. We may also procrastinate or self-sabotage in order to avoid the possibility of failure. This fear can hold us back from achieving our goals.

Embrace Failure as a Stepping Stone to Success

It's important to remember that failure is a part of life. Everyone fails at some point. The important thing is to learn from our mistakes and to keep moving forward. We can embrace failure as a stepping stone to success by:

1. Reframing Our Mindset. Instead of viewing failure as a negative event, we can view it as an opportunity to learn and grow.

2. Focusing on the Positive. When we fail, it's important to focus on the things we did well. This will help us build our confidence and move forward.

3. Celebrating Our Successes. When we achieve a goal, it's important to celebrate our success. This will help us build our self-esteem and stay motivated.

Reframing the Role of Failure in Your Journey

Failure is a part of life, but it doesn't have to define us. We can choose to view failure as a learning opportunity and a stepping stone to success. By embracing failure and learning from our mistakes, we can increase our chances of achieving our goals.

Here are some additional tips for overcoming the fear of failure:

1. Talk to Someone You Trust. Talking about your fears can help you feel less alone and more supported.

2. Set Realistic Goals. Setting small, achievable goals can help you build your confidence and avoid feeling overwhelmed.

3. Take Breaks. When you're feeling overwhelmed, take a break from your work or your studies. This will help you clear your head and come back to your task refreshed.

4. Reward Yourself for Your Successes. When you achieve a goal, reward yourself with something you enjoy and celebrate it. This will help you stay motivated and keep moving forward.

Remember, failure is not the end of the world. It's just a part of the journey. By learning from our mistakes and staying positive, we can achieve our goals.

External Validation and Self-Worth

In our modern world, seeking external validation has become the norm and a yardstick of our worthiness. We post our accomplishments on social media, seeking likes and comments to affirm our achievements. We yearn for praise at work, longing for that nod of approval from our superiors. We even gauge our self-worth by the number of followers we have or the validation we receive from others. When we base our self-worth on the opinions of others, we are setting ourselves up for disappointment and self-sabotage. This is because the opinions of others are constantly changing and are often based on factors that are beyond our control. If we rely on others to validate us, we will always be at their mercy.

How Tying Self-Worth to External Recognition Perpetuates the Cycle

When we tie our self-worth to external recognition, we are making our happiness and our sense of worth dependent on the opinions of others. This can be a very unstable foundation for our self-esteem. If we don't get the recognition we're looking for, we may feel rejected, worthless, or inadequate. This can lead to self-sabotaging behavior in an attempt to get the approval we crave.

Cultivating a Resilient Sense of Self-Worth That Is Internally Driven and Immune to External Opinions

To break the cycle of self-sabotage, we need to cultivate a resilient sense of self-worth that is internally driven and immune to external opinions. This means learning to value ourselves for who we are, not for what others think of us.

Here are some tips for cultivating a resilient sense of self-worth:

1. Identify Your Core Values. What are the things that are most important to you? What makes you feel good about yourself?

2. Focus on Your Strengths. What are you good at? What do you enjoy doing?

3. Set Realistic Goals. Don't set yourself up for failure by setting unrealistic goals.

4. Take Care of Yourself. Make sure you're getting enough sleep, eating healthy foods, and exercising regularly.

5. Spend Time with Positive People. Surround yourself with people who make you feel good about yourself.

Be kind to yourself when you make mistakes. Everyone makes mistakes.

Key Takeaways

- Childhood experiences can shape our beliefs, resulting in adult self-sabotage.

- Self-sabotage often stems from subconscious patterns rooted in childhood experiences.

- Limiting beliefs, often subconscious, are potent drivers of self-sabotage.

- Identifying and challenging limiting beliefs is essential for breaking free from self-sabotage.

- Fear, rooted in past trauma, can perpetuate self-sabotaging behaviors.

- Fear, whether of success or failure, can inhibit personal growth and reinforce self-sabotage.

- Past failures can trigger self-sabotage, leading to fear of repeating mistakes.

- Viewing past failures as opportunities for growth can help counteract their influence on self-sabotage.

- External validation can fuel self-sabotage by tethering self-worth to others' opinions.

- Shifting from external validation to intrinsic self-worth is a powerful antidote to self-sabotage.

Now that you've unraveled the root causes of self-sabotage, it's time to embark on a transformative journey of self-discovery and growth. Reflect on the insights gained from this chapter, particularly the recognition of childhood imprints, limiting beliefs, the role of fear, the impact of past failures, and the allure of external validation.

Take a moment to identify which aspects resonate most with your own experiences and understand how they may have influenced your self-sabotaging behaviors. With this newfound awareness, you're better equipped to disrupt the negative patterns that have held you back.

In the next chapter, we'll delve into practical strategies to challenge and change these negative thought patterns and beliefs, offering you tips to break free from self-sabotage's grip. Get ready to change the story you tell yourself, replace negative beliefs with positive ones, and welcome a future full of self-discovery and growth.

Part 2: Breaking the Cycle of Self-Sabotage

Chapter 3: Disrupting Negative Thought Patterns and Beliefs

"I'm not good enough. I can't do it. I'm a failure." These are just a few of the negative thoughts many of us have from time to time. But when these thoughts become persistent and pervasive, they can be very damaging to our self-esteem and confidence. They can also make it difficult to achieve our goals. If we want to live our best lives, we need to learn to disrupt these negative thoughts and beliefs.

Imagine what it would be like to live a life without these negative thoughts. Imagine feeling confident in your abilities, believing in yourself, and knowing that you can achieve anything you set your mind to. This is what it means to disrupt negative thought patterns and beliefs.

Disrupting negative thought patterns and beliefs is not easy, but it is possible. It takes time, effort, and practice. But the rewards are worth it. When you learn to disrupt your negative thoughts, you will start to see a difference in your life. You will feel more confident, motivated, and capable. You will also be more likely to achieve your goals.

So, if you are struggling with negative thoughts, don't give up. There is hope. Just continue reading, and with the techniques in this chapter, you will learn how to disrupt your negative thoughts and beliefs and start living your best life.

The Power of Self-Awareness

Self-awareness is the ability to understand one's own thoughts, feelings, and behaviors. It is the foundation of emotional intelligence and is essential for personal growth and development.

When we are self-aware, we are better able to identify our negative thought patterns and beliefs. We can then challenge these thoughts and beliefs and replace them with more positive ones.

Self-awareness also helps us understand our triggers. These are the events or situations that tend to trigger our negative thoughts and emotions. When we know our triggers, we can learn to manage them more effectively.

Importance of Self-Awareness

Self-awareness is your mental GPS. It's the ability to step back and observe your thoughts, feelings, and behaviors without judgment. When it comes to combating self-sabotage, self-awareness is your most potent weapon. Why? Because you can't fix what you can't see. Self-awareness shines a spotlight on the darkest corners of your mind, revealing the patterns that keep you stuck.

Imagine a person who is constantly late for meetings and appointments. Without self-awareness, they may brush it off as a personality trait. However, with self-awareness, they may discover that their lateness stems from a fear of confrontation or a need for attention. Knowing this, they can work on addressing the root cause of their behavior.

Self-Awareness as Your Emotional Compass

Your emotions are like signposts; they provide valuable information about your thoughts and beliefs. Self-awareness allows you to decipher these signs. For example, if you consistently feel anxious in social situations, self-awareness can help you recognize that you hold certain negative beliefs about your social skills or self-worth.

Once you pinpoint these beliefs, you can start to challenge and change them. This transformation often leads to a more positive emotional landscape, where confidence replaces anxiety and self-assurance replaces self-doubt.

Practical Exercises to Enhance Self-Awareness

Building self-awareness is like developing a muscle; it takes practice. Here are some practical exercises to get you started:

1. The Thought Diary. This is a simple but effective exercise where you write down your thoughts and feelings throughout the day. This can help you identify patterns in your thinking and identify negative thoughts that are sabotaging your success.

2. Mindfulness Meditation. Mindfulness encourages you to observe your thoughts and emotions non-judgmentally. This practice enhances your ability to step back and gain perspective.

3. Feedback from Others. Seek honest feedback from friends or family. Sometimes, others can see patterns in our behavior that we're blind to.

4. Question Your Thoughts. When you notice a negative thought, ask yourself, "Is this thought based on facts or assumptions?" Challenging your thoughts is a powerful tool for self-awareness.

5. Emotional Check-Ins. Periodically ask yourself how you're feeling and why. This simple habit can foster self-awareness in everyday life.

Rephrasing Your Inner Thoughts

Have you ever paid attention to the dialogue that plays out in your mind? The stream of thoughts that accompany you through your day, shaping your decisions, influencing your mood, and, ultimately, defining your actions? This inner conversation, often unnoticed, holds immense power over your life. In this subtopic, we'll delve into the concept of your inner dialogue, uncover its profound influence on your behavior, and equip you with strategies to transform it from a saboteur into a powerful ally.

Your inner dialogue is the narrative you have with yourself. It's the voice that comments on your experiences, offers opinions, and interprets the world around you. But what happens when this inner voice turns critical, judgmental, and negative? When it constantly reminds you of your flaws, mistakes, and limitations, it becomes a force of self-sabotage.

The journey to disrupting negative thought patterns begins with self-awareness. Start by paying attention to your inner dialogue. What is it saying? Is it filled with self-doubt, self-criticism, and self-limiting beliefs? Identifying these patterns is the first step toward change.

Transforming Negative into Empowering: Strategies That Work

1. Mindfulness Meditation. Mindfulness helps you observe your thoughts without judgment. By practicing mindfulness, you can catch negative self-talk as it arises and choose not to engage with it.

2. Affirmations. Create a list of positive affirmations that counteract your negative self-talk. Repeat these affirmations daily to reinforce empowering beliefs.

3. Cognitive Behavioral Therapy (CBT). CBT is a therapeutic approach that focuses on changing negative thought patterns. Working with a therapist trained in CBT can be highly effective in transforming your inner dialogue.

4. Self-Compassion. Treat yourself with the same kindness and understanding that you would offer to a friend. Replace self-criticism with self-compassion, acknowledging that nobody is perfect and that mistakes are opportunities for growth.

Thomas Edison. Edison faced numerous failures while inventing the light bulb. Instead of seeing these failures as setbacks, he viewed them as steps toward success, famously saying, "I have not failed. I've just found 10,000 ways that won't work."

J.K. Rowling. Before becoming one of the world's most successful authors, Rowling battled poverty and depression. She harnessed the power of her inner narrative to persevere through rejection and adversity.

These individuals go from doubt to determination, from self-criticism to self-empowerment. Their journeys demonstrate that, with awareness and the right strategies, anyone can disrupt negative thought patterns and rewrite their inner thoughts.

Embracing a Growth Mindset

A growth mindset is the belief that our abilities can be developed and improved through hard work and dedication. People with a growth mindset believe that they can learn new things, overcome challenges, and achieve their goals.

A fixed mindset, on the other hand, is the belief that our abilities are set in stone. People with a fixed mindset believe that they are born with certain talents and abilities and that they cannot change them.

A growth mindset is essential for overcoming self-sabotage. When we believe that we can learn and grow, we are more likely to take risks, try new things, and persevere in the face of challenges. Those with a growth mindset embrace challenges, persist through obstacles, and see failures as stepping stones to success. In contrast, individuals with a fixed mindset believe that their abilities are innate, leading them to avoid challenges and become disheartened by setbacks.

Why is a growth mindset crucial in the battle against self-sabotage? Because it redefines how we perceive challenges and failures. Instead of viewing them as reflections of our inadequacies, a growth mindset frames them as opportunities to grow and improve. This shift in perspective has a profound impact on how we approach our goals and navigate setbacks.

Practical Steps to Cultivate a Growth Mindset

1. Embrace Challenges. Begin by reframing challenges as opportunities to learn and grow. Embrace tasks that stretch your abilities and take you out of your comfort zone.

2. View Effort as the Path to Mastery. Understand that effort is the path to mastery. Embrace the process of learning, even when it's challenging or involves making mistakes.

3. Learn from Failures. Instead of dwelling on failures, analyze them objectively. What can you learn from this experience? How can you improve moving forward?

4. Seek Feedback and Criticism. Feedback is a valuable tool for growth. Welcome constructive criticism as an opportunity to refine your skills and knowledge.

5. Celebrate Progress. Acknowledge and celebrate your progress, no matter how small. Each step forward is a testament to your growth.

Decades of research by psychologist Carol Dweck have illuminated the power of a growth mindset. Her studies have shown that individuals with a growth mindset tend to outperform their fixed-mindset counterparts, not only in academic settings but also in professional and personal domains.

For instance, in a study involving students, those with a growth mindset were more likely to embrace challenges, persevere through difficulties, and achieve higher grades. In the workplace, employees with a growth mindset are more adaptable, resilient, and open to feedback, contributing to their professional success.

The Transformative Power of a Growth Mindset

By embracing a growth mindset, you're not merely changing your thoughts; you're rewiring your entire approach to life's challenges. Self-sabotage thrives in the soil of self-doubt and fear. A growth mindset acts as a shield, deflecting these negative influences and allowing you to forge ahead with confidence and resilience.

In the face of self-sabotage, a growth mindset whispers, "You can learn from this. You can grow stronger." It transforms setbacks into stepping stones and failures into valuable lessons. It empowers you to view challenges not as threats but as opportunities waiting to be seized.

As you continue your journey to disrupt negative thought patterns and beliefs, remember that cultivating a growth mindset is not an overnight endeavor. It's a commitment to lifelong learning and a dedication to embracing the possibilities hidden within challenges. With each step, you'll inch closer to a mindset that propels you toward personal and professional success.

The Role of Affirmations and Visualization

Affirmations and visualization are two powerful tools that can help us overcome self-sabotage. Affirmations are positive statements that we repeat to ourselves, while visualization is the practice of creating mental images of ourselves achieving our goals.

When we repeat positive affirmations, we are essentially sending messages to our subconscious mind. Over time, these messages can help to change our beliefs and attitudes, which can lead to positive changes in our behavior.

Visualization is also a powerful tool for change. When we visualize ourselves achieving our goals, we are essentially creating a blueprint for our subconscious mind to follow. This can help us stay motivated and focused on our goals.

Affirmations are like seeds planted in the fertile soil of your subconscious mind. When nurtured and repeated consistently, they can sprout into powerful beliefs that shape your reality. But not all affirmations are created equal. Effective affirmations are:

- **Positive.** They frame your goals and desires in a positive light, focusing on what you want, not what you want to avoid.

- **Present Tense.** They are crafted in the present tense as if your desired outcome is already happening.

- **Personal.** They resonate with you personally, aligning with your values and aspirations.

- **Emotionally Charged.** They evoke strong emotions, reinforcing their impact.

For example, instead of saying, "I will overcome challenges," a more effective affirmation would be, "I am resilient and confidently overcome every challenge that comes my way."

Visualization: Painting Your Mental Canvas

Visualization is the art of painting vivid mental pictures of your desired outcomes. When you vividly imagine your success, your brain interprets these mental images as real experiences, sparking a cascade of neurobiological processes that align your actions with your vision.

Imagine that you're preparing for a job interview. You can use visualization to:

- See yourself confidently answering questions.

- Feel the firm handshake of the interviewer.

- Hear the words, "You're hired."

This mental rehearsal primes your mind and body for success.

How Affirmations and Visualization Can Rewire Your Brain

Our brains are constantly changing and adapting. This process is called neuroplasticity. When we repeat positive affirmations and visualize ourselves achieving our goals, we are actually creating new neural pathways in our brains. These new neural pathways can help us think more positively and believe in ourselves, which can lead to positive changes in our behavior.

Positive affirmations are not just about saying nice things to yourself. They are a powerful tool that can help you change your thoughts, beliefs, and behaviors.

How to Craft Effective Affirmations and Visualization Routines

When crafting affirmations, it is important to use positive language and be specific. For example, instead of saying, "I am a good person," you could say, "I am kind, compassionate, and helpful."

It is also important to repeat your affirmations regularly. The more you repeat them, the more powerful they will become.

When visualizing, it is important to create vivid and detailed images of yourself achieving your goals. The more real the images feel, the more effective they will be.

You can also try to associate positive emotions with your visualizations. This will help make them even more powerful.

1. **Identify Your Goals.** Start by clearly defining your goals. What do you want to achieve or manifest in your life?

2. Craft Positive Statements. Create affirmations that align with your goals. Keep them positive, present-tense, personal, and emotionally charged.

3. Visualize Your Success. Dedicate time daily to visualization. Find a quiet space, close your eyes, and vividly imagine yourself achieving your goals. Engage all your senses to make the mental picture as real as possible.

4. Repetition is key; Consistency is Crucial. Repetition reinforces the new beliefs and mental images you're creating.

5. Use Visualization as a Complement. Combine visualization with affirmations. While you repeat affirmations, visualize them coming true. This reinforces the message.

6. Believe in Yourself. Cultivate belief in the power of these practices. Trust that they are rewiring your mind for success.

When you consistently practice positive affirmations and visualization, you begin to see a transformation. The negative thought patterns that once held you back lose their grip. You become more resilient in the face of challenges, more confident in your abilities, and more focused on your goals.

Claude Steele, a distinguished social psychologist and emeritus professor at Stanford University, introduced the groundbreaking concept of self-affirmation theory. This theory has since become a cornerstone of research within the field of social psychology, shedding profound light on human behavior and motivation.

Steele's theory revolves around the idea that individuals are inherently driven to maintain a positive self-image and self-integrity. When faced with threats to their self-esteem, such as failures or criticism, people often experience psychological discomfort. Self-affirmation theory posits that individuals can mitigate this discomfort by affirming their core values and beliefs, which serve as a psychological buffer against such threats.

This research underscores the profound impact of Claude Steele's pioneering work, demonstrating how the simple act of reaffirming one's values can foster resilience, bolster self-esteem, and enhance overall well-being.

Key Takeaways

- Self-awareness is the cornerstone of transformation, enabling you to recognize and challenge negative thought patterns.

- Rephrasing your inner dialogue is a potent tool; shift from self-doubt to self-empowerment through positive affirmations.

- Embrace a growth mindset to view challenges as opportunities for growth and learning.

- Visualizing a mental picture of yourself can reshape your reality by aligning your thoughts with your goals.

- Positive affirmations, when positive, present-tense, personal, and emotionally charged, can nurture powerful self-beliefs.

- Consistency is key; regular practice of affirmations and visualization reinforces their impact.

- Belief in the process is crucial; trust that these practices can reshape your self-esteem and confidence.

- Craft your affirmations and visualizations to align with your specific goals and aspirations.

As we conclude this transformative chapter on disrupting negative thought patterns and beliefs, you've gained essential tools to reshape your self-perception. Now, it's time to harness this newfound knowledge and embark on the next leg of your journey toward lasting self-empowerment.

The next chapter is about habit formation. Here, you'll discover how cultivating positive daily practices can reinforce your self-esteem, boost confidence, and pave the way for a more empowered you.

We'll also uncover the secrets to building lasting positive behaviors, and you will be equipped with actionable strategies to integrate these habits into your daily life effectively.

Don't miss this opportunity to continue your personal growth journey. Turn the page, and let's embark on the path to cultivating a more empowered and fulfilling life. Let's begin.

Chapter 4: Cultivating Positive Habits and Behaviors

John was a young professional who was just starting his career. He was ambitious and driven, and he wanted to achieve great things. But he was also feeling overwhelmed and stressed. There was so much to learn, and he didn't know where to start.

One day, John decided to talk to his mentor about his problems. His mentor told him about the power of positive habits. The mentor said that people who had positive habits, such as rising early, exercising regularly, eating a healthy diet, and taking proper care of themselves, were more likely to be successful in their careers.

This piqued John's interest. He decided to start practicing some positive habits, such as waking up early and meditating for 10 minutes each day.

At first, it was difficult to make these changes. John was tired, and he didn't feel like meditating. But he kept at it, and eventually, it got easier.

A few months later, John started to see a difference in his life. He was feeling more energized and focused. He was also more productive at work.

John was amazed at how much of a difference these positive habits had made in his life. He was proof that the power of positive habits was real.

John continued to practice positive habits, and he eventually achieved his dream of becoming a successful businessman. He was able to build a successful company and create a life that he loved.

Many young professionals struggle to develop good habits. But it is important to remember that good habits are essential for success. Developing good habits takes time and effort, but it is worth it. When you have good habits, you are more likely to be successful in your career. You are also more likely to be happy and fulfilled.

Cultivating a positive habit can mean signing up for a gym, starting a monthly reading challenge, or joining a support group where you can find people who inspire you to spend time with them.

In this chapter, we will explore the profound influence of habits on your personal and professional journey. You will discover the act of crafting behaviors that lead to lasting self-improvement. From understanding the habit loop to harnessing the power of keystone habits, you'll gain the tools to sculpt your life's masterpiece. Whether you seek to enhance your career, boost your self-esteem, or simply lead a more fulfilling life, this chapter will equip you with the knowledge and strategies to achieve your aspirations. One positive habit at a time will guide you towards profound self-discovery and career success.

The Habit Loop

Our habits are not as random as they seem. They are governed by a complex system of neural pathways in our brains. This system is called the habit loop.

Habits, those powerful autopilot behaviors that govern a significant portion of our daily lives, often operate in the background, shaping our actions without us even realizing it. To unlock the potential of positive habit cultivation, it's essential to decode the intricate neural pathways that underlie the habit loop.

Understanding the Cue-Routine-Reward cycle that underpins habit formation

Our brains are a complex symphony of neurons, continually firing electrical signals to communicate information. When we repeat a specific behavior or action, these signals follow a particular pathway, creating a well-trodden neural route. These neural pathways become superhighways. They're designed for efficiency, allowing us to execute routine actions with minimal cognitive effort. This is why, after some time, brushing your teeth or tying your shoelaces requires little conscious thought.

The habit loop is a powerful force in our lives. It can help us develop good habits, but it can also lead us to develop bad habits.

If we want to change our habits, we need to understand the habit loop and how it works. We need to identify the cues that trigger our bad habits, and we need to find new routines that will give us a better reward.

The essence of habit formation revolves around the cue-routine-reward cycle. Let's break it down:

- Cue: This is the trigger that initiates the habit. It can be an external prompt, an emotional state, a specific time of day, or even a particular location. Cues are the starting point of the habit loop.

- Routine: This is the actual behavior or action prompted by the cue. It's what you do in response to the trigger. If your cue is stress, your routine might be eating comfort food or biting your nails.

- Reward: After completing the routine, your brain receives a reward, typically in the form of a release of feel-good neurotransmitters like dopamine. This reinforces the habit loop, making it more likely that you'll repeat the behavior when faced with the same cue in the future.

To illustrate this cycle, consider the habit of checking your phone (routine) when you hear a notification sound (cue). The satisfaction of finding a message or interesting content (reward) reinforces the behavior, making you more likely to check your phone when it next pings.

Deconstructing Your Habits

Now that you grasp the habit loop's components, it's time to turn your attention inward. Take a closer look at your habits, both positive and negative. Consider what triggers these behaviors (the cues), what you do in response (the routines), and what satisfaction or relief you derive from them (the rewards).

For example, if you're an avid procrastinator (routine) when faced with a daunting task (cue), your brain might reward you with temporary relief from anxiety (reward). Recognizing this habit loop in your life is the first step toward reshaping it.

1. Identify the Habit. Pinpoint a specific habit you want to analyze, whether it's related to your career, health, or personal life.

2. Break It Down. Dissect the habit loop by identifying the cue, routine, and reward associated with it.

3. Question the Reward. Ask yourself what you gain from this behavior. Is the reward genuinely beneficial, or is it a short-term fix that ultimately hinders your progress?

By dissecting your habits, you gain insight into your behavior, enabling you to replace destructive routines with positive alternatives. This process sets the stage for effective habit transformation, a cornerstone of personal and professional growth.

The Power of Keystone Habits

You know when you decide to commit to a single daily habit, like exercising in the morning. Initially, it seems unrelated to your broader life goals, but watch as it seamlessly becomes part of your everyday routine, leading to a domino effect. Regular exercise leads to improved physical health, which in turn boosts your energy levels and self-confidence. This newfound confidence encourages you to pursue career opportunities you once deemed out of reach, leading to professional growth and financial stability.

This domino effect illustrates the power of keystone habits. These are habits that, when practiced consistently, initiate a chain reaction of positive changes in various areas of your life. Identifying and cultivating them is akin to finding the perfect note that harmonizes an entire symphony.

Identifying Your Personal Keystone Habits

Keystone habits are not one-size-fits-all. What serves as a keystone for one person may not hold the same transformative power for another. The key lies in self-awareness and introspection. Ask yourself:

- What areas of my life do I wish to improve?

- Are there habits I already practice that seem to positively impact multiple aspects of my life?

- What habits could potentially serve as catalysts for change?

Not all habits are created equal. Some habits are more powerful than others. These are the keystone habits that can have a big impact on your life.

Some examples of keystone habits include:

1. Exercise. Exercise is a keystone habit because it can improve your physical and mental health. It can also help you lose weight, reduce stress, and improve your mood.

2. Sleep. Sleep is another keystone habit. When you get enough sleep, you are better able to focus, learn, and make decisions. You are also less likely to get sick.

3. Meditation. Meditation is a keystone habit because it can help you reduce stress, improve your focus, and increase your self-awareness.

4. Reading. Reading is a keystone habit because it can help you learn new things, expand your knowledge, and improve your vocabulary.

5. Writing. Writing is a keystone habit because it can help you clarify your thoughts, express yourself creatively, and achieve your goals.

Crafting Your Keystone Habit Integration Plan

Once you've identified your potential keystone habits, it's time to integrate them into your daily routine. This process requires a level of strategic planning.

1. Start Smal. Begin with a single keystone habit. Trying to adopt too many new habits simultaneously can lead to overwhelm and decreased chances of success.

2. Set Clear Goals. Define precisely what you want to achieve with your keystone habit. Make your goals SMART (Specific, Measurable, Achievable, Relevant, Time-bound).

3. Create a Routine. Establish a consistent time and place for your habit. Consistency is the key to forming lasting habits.

4. Track Your Progress. Use a journal or habit-tracking app to monitor your consistency and progress. This not only keeps you accountable but also provides a visual record of your success.

5. Leverage Triggers. Associate your keystone habit with an existing habit or a specific cue in your daily routine. This makes it easier to remember and integrate.

6. Stay Patient. Habit formation takes time. Be patient with yourself and recognize that setbacks are a natural part of the process.

By identifying your unique keystone habits and integrating them systematically, you're taking a giant step towards crafting the symphony of your life. These small yet mighty habits are the notes that harmonize your personal and professional growth, helping you reach your goals and aspirations.

The power of keystone habits is real. By identifying and focusing on these habits, you can create positive changes in all areas of your life.

Here are some additional insights and practical advice for identifying and integrating keystone habits into your life:

- Pay attention to the habits that seem to have a positive impact on your life. These are the habits that you may want to focus on.

- Experiment with different habits and see what works best for you. There is no one-size-fits-all approach to keystone habits.

- Be willing to change your habits as needed. Your needs and goals may change over time, so be willing to adjust your habits accordingly.

- Don't be afraid to ask for help. If you are struggling to change your habits, talk to a friend, family member, or therapist.

Creating a Habit-Formation Strategy

Creating a Habit-Formation Strategy involves understanding the inner workings of habits, crafting a plan that harmonizes with your life, and using the SMART goals framework to fine-tune your progress.

The Psychology of habit stacking and implementation intentions

Habit stacking and implementation intentions are two powerful techniques that can help you form new habits.

Habit stacking is the practice of linking a new habit to an existing one. For example, you could stack the habit of reading before bed with the habit of brushing your teeth.

Implementation intentions are a specific type of goal setting that helps you overcome the obstacles that stand in the way of your goals. For example, you could make it your intention to read for 30 minutes every day after you wake up.

Forging a Well-Structured Roadmap

Like a conductor guiding a symphony, you need a roadmap to direct your habit-building journey. Here's how to craft one:

1. Identify Your Desired Habits. Begin by listing the habits you wish to cultivate. Ensure they align with your personal and career goals.

2. Set Priorities. Not all habits are created equal. Prioritize those with the most significant impact on your objectives.

3. Break It Down. Divide your habits into smaller, manageable steps. This prevents overwhelm and fosters a sense of accomplishment.

4. Create a Schedule. Determine when and how often you'll practice each habit. Consistency is key.

5. Visualize Success. Mentally rehearse your habit's execution. Visualization strengthens your commitment.

6. Implement Habit Stacking. Attach new habits to existing routines to simplify integration.

7. Accountability. Share your habit goals with a trusted friend or mentor who can provide support and encouragement.

8. Track Your Progress. Maintain a habit journal or use habit-tracking apps to monitor your consistency.

Employing SMART Goals Framework

The SMART goals framework is a popular way to set goals that are specific, measurable, achievable, relevant, and time-bound.

When you use the SMART goals framework to set goals for your habit formation, you are more likely to achieve your goals.

Here are some examples of SMART goals for habit formation:

- **Specific:** Define your habit clearly. Instead of "exercise more," specify "I will jog for 30 minutes every morning."

- **Measurable:** Establish criteria for tracking progress. For instance, you might measure exercise by the number of days or minutes.

- **Achievable:** Ensure your habit is realistically attainable. Setting overly ambitious goals can lead to frustration.

- **Relevant:** Ensure your habit aligns with your broader goals, whether personal or career-oriented.

- **Time-bound:** Set a deadline for achieving your habit. This creates a sense of urgency and commitment.

By understanding the psychology of habit stacking, crafting a well-structured roadmap, and employing SMART goals, you'll set up a symphony of positive behaviors that lead to lasting self-improvement. The stage is set for you to compose the masterpiece of your life, one habit at a time.

Overcoming Pitfalls

Setbacks are a natural part of the habit-building process. Just as a virtuoso may hit the wrong note during a performance, you, too, will encounter moments where your positive habit routine falters. These setbacks often take various forms:

1. Time Constraints: The demands of a busy life can derail your well-intentioned habit-building efforts. Work, family, and unexpected responsibilities can consume your time and energy.

2. Lack of Motivation: There will be days when motivation wanes. You may wake up feeling uninspired, making it tempting to skip your habit practice.

3. Procrastination: The siren call of procrastination can be deafening. It lulls you into believing that tomorrow is a better day to restart your positive habit journey.

4. External Factors: Sometimes, external factors beyond your control come into play. Illness, a family crisis, or a sudden change in circumstances can disrupt your routine.

Strategies for Resilience

In the world of habit formation, setbacks are not a sign of failure but rather an opportunity for growth. Embracing these challenges is a critical aspect of sustaining your positive habits.

Here are some strategies to help you navigate setbacks:

1. Anticipate and Plan. Recognize that setbacks are a part of the journey. Prepare for them by creating a contingency plan for when life throws a curveball. Having a backup strategy in place can help you stay on track.

2. Practice Self-Compassion. Just as a soothing interlude softens a symphony's crescendo, self-compassion offers solace in moments of falter. Instead of berating yourself for a missed day, acknowledge the setback with kindness and resolve to continue.

3. Mindful Adaptation. Be flexible in your approach. If you miss a day of your habit, don't abandon it altogether. Adjust and continue with your plan rather than succumbing to all-or-nothing thinking.

4. Accountability. Share your habit-building journey with a friend or a mentor who can provide support and hold you accountable. Knowing someone is rooting for your success can be a powerful motivator.

5. Celebrate Small Wins. Acknowledge and celebrate your successes, no matter how minor. These victories reinforce your commitment and provide motivation to persevere.

6. Revisit Your Why. Remind yourself of the reasons behind your habit-building efforts. Reconnecting with your 'why' can reignite your motivation during challenging times.

Everyone makes mistakes. When you slip up and fall back into old habits, don't beat yourself up about it. Instead, practice self-compassion.

Self-compassion is the practice of being kind and understanding to yourself, just as you would be to a friend. When you practice self-compassion, you are more likely to forgive yourself for your mistakes and get back on track.

Sustaining Habits for Long-term Success

Once you have formed new habits, it is important to sustain them for long-term success.

Here are some techniques that can help you sustain your habits:

- Self-reinforcement: Self-reinforcement is the practice of rewarding yourself for your progress. This can help you stay motivated and on track.

- Diligence tracking: Tracking your progress can help you see how far you have come and stay motivated to keep going.

- Resilience: Resilience is the ability to bounce back from setbacks. When you experience a setback, don't give up. Just pick yourself up and keep going.

Self-Reinforcement

Think of your habits as delicate blooms in a garden. They require consistent care and nourishment to thrive. Self-reinforcement is the art of nurturing these habits, ensuring they continue to blossom.

1. Tracking Progress. One of the most effective ways to self-reinforce is by tracking your progress. This isn't just about checking a box; it's about celebrating your victories, however small they may seem. Each checkmark is a note in your symphony of success.

2. Accountability. Share your journey with a friend or mentor who can hold you accountable. The knowledge that someone is watching can be a powerful motivator.

3. Visual Reminders. Surround yourself with visual cues that remind you of your commitment. Whether it's a vision board, sticky notes, or a daily journal, these reminders help keep your habits front and center in your mind.

Some moments are smooth, like a gentle adagio, while others are turbulent, like a tumultuous crescendo. To sustain your habits through these variations, you must cultivate resilience.

- Flexibility: Resilience isn't about being rigid; it's about being flexible. Understand that there will be days when your routine is disrupted, and that's perfectly okay. What matters is your ability to adapt and get back on track.

- Learn from Setbacks: Every setback is a learning opportunity. Instead of chastising yourself, analyze what led to the slip and how you can prevent it in the future. It's not about perfection; it's about progress.

- The Power of Self-Compassion: Self-compassion is your greatest ally in maintaining habits. Just as a musician doesn't berate themselves for missing a note in a complex composition, you shouldn't berate yourself for a momentary lapse. Be kind to yourself and recognize that you're on a journey of growth.

Key Takeaways

- Habits are driven by a cue-routine-reward loop; understanding and modifying this loop is essential for habit change.

- Small changes, like keystone habits, can have a profound impact on your life by creating a domino effect of positive change.

- Employ psychological techniques and SMART goals to create a structured and effective habit-formation strategy.

- Embrace setbacks and failures as valuable lessons, using them as stepping stones to progress.

- Self-reinforcement techniques like progress tracking, visual reminders, and accountability are crucial for maintaining positive habits. Consistently reinforcing your efforts keeps you motivated.

- Practice self-reinforcement through tracking and accountability, and develop resilience and self-compassion to maintain habits through life's changes.

- Life is unpredictable. Learning to be flexible and adapt to changing circumstances without abandoning your habits is a valuable skill. Understand that deviations happen, but they don't have to derail your progress.

- Setbacks are not failures; they are opportunities to learn and grow. Analyze what went wrong, adjust your approach, and use setbacks as stepping stones toward improvement.

- Be kind to yourself. Self-compassion is a powerful tool for maintaining habits. Treat yourself with the same understanding and forgiveness you would offer a friend when things don't go as planned.

As you conclude this chapter, equipped with the knowledge and strategies to nurture positive habits, your journey toward self-improvement and success is well underway. However, there's more to explore in your quest for personal and professional growth.

The next chapter delves deeper into the emotional aspects of your journey. Resilience, the ability to bounce back from adversity, and self-compassion, the practice of being kind to yourself, are essential tools in your toolkit. In this chapter, you'll learn how to cultivate resilience to overcome life's challenges and embrace self-compassion as a guiding force in your pursuit of excellence.

Reflect on your journey so far. Where have you encountered setbacks, and how have you handled them? Consider how you typically respond to your own mistakes and failures. Are you self-critical or self-compassionate? Prepare to explore and embrace the emotional side of self-improvement in the upcoming chapter.

The next chapter promises to be transformative.

Chapter 5: Building Resilience and Self-Compassion

Just like an athlete who has been preparing for a big competition. He has been working tirelessly for months, but he is still nervous. He realizes that this is his chance to shine and make his dreams come true.

He is feeling confident as competition day approaches. He has done everything he can to prepare and is ready to give it his all. But when the competition started, he made a mistake. He misses a crucial shot and loses the first round.

He is disappointed, but he is not giving up. He understands that he cannot change the past, but he can influence the future. He continued to train and work hard, and he eventually won the next competition.

The athlete possesses a resilient mind. Resilience can help us achieve our goals. When we experience setbacks, it is easy to give up. But if we have resilience, we can overcome these setbacks and keep going.

This chapter explores the essence of resilience and self-compassion, offering you the tools to overcome setbacks, embrace self-kindness, and emerge from life's challenges stronger and more determined than ever. In this chapter, you, too, will find insights, strategies, and practical advice to navigate your own journey with resilience and self-compassion.

The Essence of Resilience

Resilience is the ability to bounce back from setbacks. It is the ability to overcome challenges and keep going. Resilience is crucial for success because it allows us to persevere in the face of adversity.

Resilience, at its core, is the ability to withstand, adapt to, and grow from challenges. It's not merely about surviving; it's about thriving despite the challenges life throws your way.

Consider Abraham Lincoln, one of America's greatest presidents. He faced countless failures and defeats on his journey to leadership, yet his resilience carried him through. Lincoln's story exemplifies that resilience is not an innate trait; it's a skill that can be developed and honed.

Abraham Lincoln's life is a remarkable testament to the power of resilience. Before becoming the 16th President of the United States and leading the nation through one of its most challenging periods, Lincoln endured a series of personal and professional setbacks that could have broken a less resilient spirit.

Lincoln grew up in poverty with limited access to formal education. He lost his mother to milk sickness when he was just nine years old, and his family moved frequently, struggling to make ends meet. His business ventures failed, leading him into bankruptcy. He experienced the loss of a sweetheart, the death of a child, and a turbulent marriage. His early forays into politics were met with defeat, including an unsuccessful run for the U.S. Senate.

Perhaps the most daunting challenge Lincoln faced was the Civil War, a conflict that tore the nation apart. He endured criticism, political turmoil, and the immense burden of making life-and-death decisions for the country. Yet, through it all, Lincoln displayed unyielding resolve and an unwavering commitment to preserving the Union and abolishing slavery.

What makes Lincoln's story so compelling is that he didn't start his life's journey with an innate gift of resilience. Instead, he developed it over time through a combination of factors, including self-reflection, a growth mindset, and an unshakable belief in his ability to make a difference.

Lincoln's experiences and failures served as stepping stones rather than stumbling blocks. He learned from each setback, adapted to changing circumstances, and maintained a deep sense of purpose. This journey of personal growth and resilience ultimately culminated in his becoming one of the most revered figures in American history.

The lesson from Lincoln's life is clear: resilience is not a fixed trait but a skill that can be cultivated through adversity and self-discovery. It's the capacity to bounce back, learn, and grow stronger, regardless of life's challenges. Lincoln's story serves as a powerful reminder that no matter where you are in your own journey, resilience can be nurtured and developed, enabling you to overcome obstacles and achieve your goals.

Researchers have found that when we face challenges, our brains can rewire themselves, forging new neural pathways that enable us to cope more effectively.

Studies have also shown that resilience can be cultivated through specific practices. Positive psychology, a field dedicated to understanding human well-being, has explored the traits and habits that foster resilience. Traits such as optimism, self-efficacy, and a growth mindset are key components of resilience.

Cultivating Resilience

So, how can you cultivate resilience in your own life? It begins with understanding that setbacks and challenges are not the end but opportunities for growth. As defined by psychologist Carol Dweck, adopting a growth mindset entails viewing failures as an opportunity to grow.

Additionally, fostering a strong support system can enhance resilience. Just as a tree with deep roots is less likely to be uprooted in a storm, individuals with strong social connections are better equipped to weather life's challenges.

Practical steps for cultivating resilience include:

1. Self-Reflection. Take time to reflect on your past challenges and how you've overcome them. Recognize your inner strength.

2. Adaptability. Be open to change and embrace new ways of thinking and doing things.

3. Positive Self-Talk. Challenge negative thoughts and replace them with affirmations that encourage self-belief.

4. Seeking Support. Lean on friends, family, or a therapist when needed. Don't hesitate to ask for help.

5. Maintaining Well-Being. Prioritize self-care through exercise, a healthy diet, and adequate sleep.

On the journey of life, resilience is your trusted companion, helping you weather the storms and emerge stronger on the other side. It's not a quality reserved for a select few; it's a skill that anyone can develop.

Navigating Life's Storms

Life is full of challenges and setbacks. When we experience these challenges, it can be difficult to know how to cope.

It's normal to feel overwhelmed, sad, angry, or scared when we experience adversity.

When we experience a challenge, it can be difficult to know how to cope. We may feel overwhelmed, stressed, or even hopeless. We may not know what to do or where to turn.

Life's storms are a part of the human experience. Whether it's a sudden job loss, a health scare, or a personal relationship breakdown, we all encounter turbulence along our journey.

These storms can be emotionally tumultuous, causing stress, anxiety, and self-doubt. However, they are also opportunities for growth, resilience, and self-discovery. How we weather these storms defines our character and shapes our future.

It is normal to feel a range of emotions when we experience adversity. Don't try to bottle up your emotions. Allow yourself to feel them and express them in a healthy way; just know that they are temporary.

Practical Strategies for Coping

1. Maintain Perspective. When faced with adversity, it's easy to become overwhelmed by negative emotions. One of the most effective strategies is to maintain perspective. Ask yourself, "Will this matter a year from now?" Often, the answer is no, and this realization can provide solace.

2. Practice Mindfulness. Mindfulness techniques, such as meditation and deep breathing, can help you stay grounded during difficult times. They allow you to observe your thoughts and emotions without judgment, reducing their impact on your well-being.

3. Seek Support. Don't bear the weight of life's storms alone. Reach out to friends, family, or a therapist for support and perspective. Talking through your challenges can provide clarity and comfort.

4. Set Realistic Goals. When facing adversity, break your challenges into smaller, manageable goals. This not only makes the path forward clearer but also provides a sense of achievement as you make progress.

5. Embrace Resilience as a Skill. Resilience is not an innate trait but a skill that can be developed. It involves adapting to adversity, learning from setbacks, and growing stronger through the process. Approach life's storms as opportunities to hone your resilience.

Maintaining Composure and Focus

Amid life's storms, maintaining composure and focus can be a Herculean task. It's easy to succumb to panic, despair, or distraction. However, these moments also hold the potential for clarity and determination.

1. Focus on Yourself. In the midst of a storm, take a moment to center yourself. Close your eyes, take deep breaths, and focus on the present moment. This simple practice can help you regain composure and make better decisions.

2. Accept Your Emotions. It's okay to feel fear, anger, or sadness during challenging times. Allow yourself to experience these emotions without judgment. Acceptance can help you process and move through them.

3. Set Priorities. In a crisis, it's essential to identify your priorities. What must be addressed immediately, and what can wait? Create a list of tasks and tackle them one at a time, starting with the most critical.

4. Seek Solitude When Needed. While support is valuable, there are moments when solitude can provide clarity. Find a quiet space to reflect, journal your thoughts, and make decisions from a place of inner calm.

Navigating life's storms is a skill that, when honed, can turn adversity into opportunity.

The Importance of Self-Compassion

Self-compassion is the practice of being kind and understanding to ourselves in the same way that we would be to a friend. It is about accepting our flaws and mistakes without judgment and giving ourselves the same care and support that we would give to others.

Self-compassion is a vital skill because it can help us cope with difficult emotions, bounce back from setbacks, and build resilience. When we have self-compassion, we are less likely to be overcome by negative emotions and more likely to take care of ourselves.

Understanding Self-Compassion

Before we unravel its significance, let's dissect what self-compassion truly entails. Dr. Kristin Neff, a pioneer in self-compassion research, identifies three core components:

- Self-Kindness: Treating yourself with warmth and understanding rather than harsh criticism when you make mistakes or face shortcomings.

- Common Humanity: Recognizing that suffering and setbacks are part of the shared human experience. You're not alone in your struggles; they are woven into the tapestry of human existence.

- Mindfulness: Approaching your pain or difficulties with a mindful, non-judgmental awareness. This involves acknowledging your emotions without over-identifying with them.

Why Self-Compassion Matters

- Resilience in the Face of Failure: Picture a scenario where you've given your all to a project, yet it doesn't yield the expected results. Without self-compassion, you might berate yourself, perpetuating negative self-talk. But when self-compassion is in play, you respond to failure with self-kindness. This, in turn, buffers the emotional blow, allowing you to bounce back quicker.

- Enhanced Emotional Well-Being: Self-compassion acts as an emotional safety net. It helps you navigate the treacherous waters of self-doubt and criticism by fostering a more positive self-image. Research suggests that self-compassionate individuals experience lower levels of anxiety, depression, and stress.

- Motivation and Goal Pursuit: Contrary to the misconception that self-compassion leads to complacency, studies show that it's a potent motivator. When you know you can rely on your own self-compassion, you're more inclined to take risks, learn from failures, and persist in the face of challenges.

Cultivating Self-Compassion

Now that we've established why self-compassion is indispensable let's delve into practical techniques to cultivate it in your daily life:

1. Self-Compassionate Self-Talk. Pay attention to your inner dialogue. When faced with self-criticism, pause and ask yourself, "What would I say to a friend in this situation?" Then, offer yourself those same comforting words.

2. Mindfulness Meditation. Engage in mindfulness practices to become more aware of your thoughts and emotions. This awareness is the first step toward self-compassion.

3. Write a Self-Compassion Letter. Imagine writing a letter to yourself as if you were comforting a dear friend going through a tough time. Express your understanding, kindness, and support.

4. Embrace Imperfection. Accept that perfection is an unattainable ideal. Embrace your flaws and vulnerabilities as part of what makes you beautifully human.

5. Seek Self-Compassion Role Models. Identify people in your life or public figures who embody self-compassion. Learn from their examples and how they respond to setbacks with kindness.

Remember, self-compassion is not a destination but a practice. It's the gentle hand that guides you through life's storms, reminding you that you are deserving of love and understanding, especially from yourself.

Embracing Failure as a Stepping Stone

Failure is a word that often carries a heavy weight, laden with disappointment and shame. But what if we dared to view it differently? What if we saw failure not as a dead end but as a stepping stone on the path to success?

Failure is a part of life. Everyone experiences failure at some point. But how we view failure can make all the difference. If we see failure as an endpoint, it can be discouraging and demoralizing. But if we see failure as a stepping stone, it can be an opportunity to learn and grow.

Learning from Failure

Failure is a remarkable teacher. It shows us what doesn't work, steering us toward more effective approaches. In this sense, every failure is a step forward, not backward. When we shift our perspective and embrace failure as a natural part of the journey, its grip on our confidence begins to loosen.

Turning Failure into Success

History is replete with stories of individuals who turned their failures into spectacular successes. J.K. Rowling, the beloved author of the Harry Potter series, faced numerous rejections from publishers before finding success. Her story reminds us that rejection and failure can be stepping stones to achieving our dreams.

Walt Disney, the creator of an empire built on dreams, was fired from a newspaper for a lack of creativity and told he lacked good ideas. Yet he persisted and went on to become an iconic figure in the world of entertainment.

Strategies for Embracing Failure

1. Reframe Your Mindset. Instead of seeing failure as final, reframe it as feedback. What can you learn from this experience? How can you use it to your advantage?

2. Celebrate Small Wins. Break your goals into smaller, more achievable steps. Celebrate each small success along the way, knowing that even if you stumble, you're still moving forward.

3. Seek Inspiration. Read about the failures and successes of others. Knowing that even the most accomplished individuals face setbacks can provide motivation to persevere.

4. Develop Resilience. Resilience is the ability to bounce back from adversity. Cultivate this skill by facing challenges head-on and learning from each experience.

5. Maintain Self-Compassion. Be kind to yourself in the face of failure. Self-compassion enables you to pick yourself up and continue your journey with a sense of worthiness.

Embrace Your Journey

In the grand tapestry of life, failure isn't a tear but a thread woven into the intricate design of your story. It's a reminder that every stumble and every setback brings you closer to your ultimate destination.

So, the next time you face failure, remember that failure isn't the end; it's your stepping stone to success.

Key Takeaways

- Resilience is the ability to bounce back from adversity and is a critical component of personal and professional growth.

- Self-compassion is about being kind and understanding toward yourself, especially during challenging times.

- Embracing failure as a stepping stone can lead to personal and professional growth.

- Resilience and self-compassion are not just theoretical concepts; they can be applied in practical ways to enhance your life.

- Practice self-compassion in your daily life by treating yourself with kindness, especially in moments of self-doubt.

- Failure isn't the opposite of success; it's a part of the journey. Embrace it as a stepping stone to growth.

- Failure offers feedback on what doesn't work, guiding you toward more effective approaches.

- Building resilience is an ongoing journey that involves facing challenges head-on and learning from each experience.

Now that we've come to the end of this chapter take a few moments each day to reflect on your experiences, embracing both successes and setbacks with self-compassion. Incorporate positive affirmations into your daily routine. Remind yourself of your worthiness and potential.

Whenever you face a setback, ask yourself, "What can I learn from this?" Use failure as a stepping stone to success.

In the next chapter, we'll explore the vital role of a support system in your journey. Learn how to cultivate meaningful connections and create a network that bolsters your success. Together, we'll uncover the power of collaboration and community on your path to achieving your dreams.

Chapter 6: Building a Support System for Success

Have you ever seen a flower push through a crack in the pavement, reaching for the sun's embrace? It's a reminder that even in the harshest conditions, life finds a way to flourish.

The flower is surrounded by concrete and asphalt, but it continues to bloom. It pushes upwards, its tender shoots breaking through the hard, unyielding surface to seek nourishment and light. It is a symbol of hope and resilience.

Much like that resilient flower, your journey through life is filled with its share of challenges and obstacles, often appearing as unyielding as that concrete pavement. Yet, despite the odds, you have the innate ability to not only survive but thrive.

If you are facing a challenge in your life, with hard work and determination, you can overcome it.

And when you do, you will be stronger and more resilient than ever before. You will be like the flower, pushing through the cracks and reaching for the sun.

This chapter is your gateway to understanding the profound impact of a support system on your path to success. We will delve into the symbiotic nature of support, exploring the ways it elevates both you and those who stand by your side. Together, we'll uncover the art of nurturing relationships, building a network of mentors and allies, and harnessing the collective power of a support system.

In this chapter, we embark on a journey to strengthen the foundations of your success. This chapter isn't just about assembling the elements of support; it's about recognizing the pivotal role that a well-structured support system plays in your pursuit of success. As we delve into the intricacies of this process, you'll discover how to foster relationships, leverage resources, and cultivate a network that propels you toward your goals.

Remember, success is rarely a solitary endeavor; it thrives within an ecosystem of support and encouragement. As we explore the art of building a healthy support system, envision yourself building a sturdy platform for your ambitions, one that will elevate you to the heights of achievement you aspire to reach.

The Power of Networking

When it comes to personal and professional growth, there's an essential tool that often goes underestimated - networking. It's more than just business cards and LinkedIn connections; it's the art of building meaningful relationships that can elevate you to new heights.

At its core, networking is about collaboration and partnership. It's the realization that we're stronger when we work together, drawing from each other's strengths and experiences. Imagine a puzzle - each piece is unique, but when they come together, they create a stunning picture.

Networking is a powerful tool that can be used to connect with people who have the skills, knowledge, and resources you need to succeed.

There are many real-life examples of successful partnerships that have been formed through networking. Here are a few:

- **Steve Jobs and Steve Wozniak:** Steve Jobs and Steve Wozniak met through a computer club at Stanford University. They collaborated to found Apple Computer, which went on to become one of the most successful companies in the world.

- **Mark Zuckerberg and Eduardo Saverin:** Mark Zuckerberg and Eduardo Saverin met at Harvard University. They collaborated to found Facebook, which is now one of the most popular social media platforms in the world.

- **Oprah Winfrey and Gayle King:** Oprah Winfrey and Gayle King met while working at a local TV station in Baltimore, Maryland. They have been friends ever since and have collaborated on many projects, including the Oprah Winfrey Show and the OWN Network.

- **Arianna Huffington and Kenneth Lerer:** Arianna Huffington and Kenneth Lerer met at a dinner party in New York City. They were both interested in starting a new media company. They collaborated to found The Huffington Post, which is now one of the most popular news websites in the world.

- **Sergey Brin and Larry Page:** Sergey Brin and Larry Page met at Stanford University. They were both working on a research project on search engines. They collaborated to develop the PageRank algorithm, which is the basis for Google's search engine.

- **Bill Gates and Melinda Gates:** Bill Gates and Melinda Gates met while working at Microsoft. They collaborated to found the Bill & Melinda Gates Foundation, which is one of the largest philanthropic organizations in the world.

Networking is more than just collecting contacts. It's about sharing knowledge, experiences, and opportunities. When you collaborate with others, you can tap into their expertise, gain fresh perspectives, and open doors to new possibilities.

Practical Networking Tips

1. Authenticity. Be genuine in your interactions. Authenticity builds trust and stronger connections.

2. Listen Actively. Pay attention to others and show a genuine interest in their stories and ideas.

3. Give Before You Get. Offer help and support without expecting immediate returns. The goodwill you create often comes back tenfold.

4. Diversify Your Network. Connect with people from various backgrounds and industries. Diversity brings different perspectives to the table.

5. Follow-Up. After initial meetings, maintain contact. Consistent communication nurtures relationships.

Networking Beyond Business

Networking isn't confined to boardrooms and corporate events. It's a life skill that extends to personal growth, too. Surrounding yourself with friends and mentors who share your interests and passions can provide the support and inspiration needed to flourish.

As we journey through this chapter, remember that networking isn't just a checkbox on your career to-do list. It's a powerful tool that can connect you with the people, ideas, and opportunities that will help you reach your fullest potential. It's about understanding that together, we can achieve more than we ever could alone.

Nurturing Meaningful Relationships

Meaningful relationships are essential for a happy and fulfilling life. They can provide us with love, support, and a sense of belonging. They can also help us grow and learn as individuals.

Like a mosaic, relationships are the colorful tiles that form its patterns and shapes. We all know relationships are important, but it's the quality of these connections, not their quantity, that truly matters.

Understand the difference between transactional and transformative relationships and how to foster the latter

Transactional relationships are those that are based on exchanging favors or goods. They are often superficial and do not provide much emotional support. Transformative relationships, on the other hand, are those that are based on mutual understanding, respect, and trust. They can provide us with deep emotional support and help us grow as individuals.

The Building Blocks of Meaningful Relationships

1. **Authenticity.** The cornerstone of any meaningful relationship is authenticity. Be yourself, and encourage others to do the same. Authenticity breeds trust and emotional intimacy.

2. Empathy. Understanding another person's perspective, feeling their emotions, and showing empathy are crucial. It's the bridge that connects hearts.

3. Effective Communication. Communication isn't just about words; it's about active listening, asking meaningful questions, and fostering open dialogue.

4. Shared Values and Interests. While opposites may attract, shared values and interests provide a solid foundation. They create common ground and ignite shared passions.

Nurturing Transformative Relationships

Transformative relationships are like gardens. They require care, attention, and patience. Here's how you can nurture them:

1. Invest Time. Meaningful connections need time to grow. Dedicate time to building and maintaining relationships.

2. Practice Vulnerability. Opening up and being vulnerable can be challenging, but it's a powerful way to deepen connections. It invites reciprocation and fosters trust.

3. Seek Growth Together. Transformative relationships often revolve around mutual personal growth. Encourage each other's dreams, provide constructive feedback, and celebrate successes together.

4. Resolve Conflicts Gracefully. Conflict is natural in any relationship. What matters is how you handle it. Approach conflict with empathy, active listening, and a commitment to finding common ground.

Meaningful relationships are a precious gift. They can enrich our lives in so many ways. By following these tips, you can nurture meaningful relationships that will last a lifetime.

Mentors and Allies: Your Guiding Lights

In the quest for success, the adage "no one is an island" holds true. Mentors and allies are people who can provide guidance, support, and encouragement on your journey to success. They can help you see your strengths and weaknesses, set goals, and develop strategies for achieving them. They can also provide you with emotional support when you need it most. Mentors and allies are the guiding lights that illuminate the path, offering insights, wisdom, and support.

Why Mentors and Allies Matter

Imagine embarking on a mountain climb without a guide, a seasoned mountaineer who knows the terrain, weather patterns, and rough paths. The journey might be possible, but it's fraught with unnecessary risks and uncertainty. Now imagine that same climb with a knowledgeable guide by your side.

Mentors are individuals who have walked the path you aspire to tread. They can provide insights, advice, and guidance based on their own experiences. Their role is not to give you all the answers but to empower you with the knowledge and perspective needed to make informed decisions.

Finding the Right Mentor

Finding a mentor may seem daunting, but it's a journey worth embarking on. Consider the following steps:

1. Identify Your Goals. Clearly define your objectives and what you hope to gain from mentorship.

2. Research Potential Mentors. Look for individuals who have achieved what you aspire to achieve. This could be within your organization, industry, or field of interest.

3. Initiate Connections. Reach out with a thoughtful message expressing your admiration for their work and your interest in learning from them.

4. Build a Relationship. As the relationship develops, invest time in building rapport and demonstrating your commitment to growth.

The Power of Allies

Allies are individuals who align with your goals and provide support, encouragement, and sometimes a fresh perspective. While they may not have walked the exact same path as your mentors, their support can be instrumental in your journey.

Cultivating Allyships

Building alliances requires authenticity, reciprocity, and a willingness to contribute to others' success as well. Here's how to foster meaningful alliances:

1. Shared Values. Identify individuals who share your values and aspirations.

2. Effective Communication. Foster open, honest, and constructive communication with potential allies.

3. Reciprocity. Remember that allyship is a two-way street. Be ready to support and uplift your allies in return.

4. Networking. Attend events, conferences, and gatherings related to your field to connect with potential allies.

The Benefits of Mentorship and Alliances

1. Accelerated Learning. Gain insights and knowledge that might take years to acquire independently.

2. Networking Opportunities. Expand your network through your mentor's or ally's connections.

3. Increased Confidence. Receive validation and encouragement from those who believe in your potential.

4. Constructive Feedback. Benefit from constructive criticism and guidance that fuels personal and professional growth.

5. New Skills and Knowledge. Mentors can share their knowledge and expertise with you.

Mentors and allies are not just role models; they are catalysts for your success. Whether you're navigating the complexities of a career, launching a new business, or seeking personal growth, their guidance and support can make the journey smoother and more fulfilling.

The Power of Giving Back

Imagine a world where every action is met with kindness and where support flows freely in a never-ending cycle of goodwill. This is the world of giving back, a place where your acts of kindness not only uplift others but also propel your own growth and success.

The reciprocity of support is the idea that when we give to others, we are also giving to ourselves. When we help others, it makes us feel good, and it also makes us more likely to be helped in the future. This is because people are more likely to help those who have helped them in the past.

Fueling Your Growth and Success

The act of giving back isn't just a one-way street. It's a dynamic exchange that nurtures your own growth and success. Here's how:

1. Enhanced Well-Being. Numerous studies have shown that acts of kindness trigger the release of feel-good hormones like oxytocin. This not only boosts your mood but also enhances your overall well-being.

2. Expanded Networks. As you engage in charitable activities or offer your expertise to others, you naturally expand your network. These connections can open doors to new opportunities and collaborations.

3. Skill Development. Volunteering or mentoring provides a platform to hone and showcase your skills. It's a chance to practice leadership, communication, and problem-solving in real-world situations.

4. Enhanced Perspective. Giving back exposes you to different perspectives and challenges, broadening your horizons and fostering empathy and understanding.

5. Sense of Fulfillment: The intrinsic reward of knowing you've made a positive impact on someone's life can be immeasurable. This sense of fulfillment is a powerful motivator.

Practical Steps to Give Back

1. Volunteer. Dedicate your time and skills to a cause or organization you're passionate about.

2. Mentorship. Share your knowledge and experience with someone who can benefit from your guidance.

3. Random Acts of Kindness. Small gestures, like buying coffee for a stranger or helping a neighbor, can brighten someone's day.

4. Philanthropy. Contribute to charitable organizations aligned with your values.

5. Community Engagement. Get involved in your local community through clean-up drives, food banks, or other initiatives.

Remember, giving back doesn't require grand gestures. It can be as simple as lending a listening ear or offering a helping hand to someone.

Creating Your Support System

A support system is a network of people who can provide you with support, guidance, and encouragement on your journey to success. It could include your family, friends, mentors, colleagues, and even strangers.

Building a strong support system is essential for achieving your dreams. It can help you stay motivated, overcome challenges, and reach your goals.

Steps to building a robust support system

1. Identify Your Needs. Begin by identifying what kind of support you need. Is it guidance, motivation, financial assistance, or emotional support? Understanding your needs is the first step in creating an effective system.

2. Seeking Guidance. Reach out to mentors and advisors who can provide valuable insights and advice based on their experiences. They can help you navigate challenges and make informed decisions.

3. Building a Network. Expand your network by attending industry events, conferences, and networking gatherings. These connections can open doors to opportunities you might not have discovered otherwise.

4. Embrace Diverse Perspectives. Your ecosystem should be diverse in terms of backgrounds, experiences, and perspectives. Embracing diversity not only enriches your support but also broadens your horizons.

5. Give and Receive. Remember that support is a two-way street. Offer help and assistance to others in your network just as you receive it. Building reciprocity strengthens your relationships.

Nurturing and Leveraging Your System

Building your support system is not a one-time endeavor; it's an ongoing process that requires nurturing and leverage. Here's how to ensure your system remains robust:

1. Regular Check-Ups. Stay connected with your mentors, advisors, and peers. Regular check-ins help maintain the connection and allow for updates and feedback.

2. Feedback Loop. Be open to feedback from your support network. Constructive criticism can be a powerful tool for growth.

3. Leverage Opportunities. Actively seek opportunities within your network, whether it's for collaboration, projects, or personal growth endeavors.

4. Adapt and Expand. As your goals evolve, so should your support system. Be willing to adapt and expand to accommodate your changing needs.

5. Gratitude and Recognition. Don't forget to express gratitude to those who have supported you. Recognizing their contributions strengthens your relationships.

Your support system is a dynamic force in your life. When nurtured and leveraged effectively, it can be the wind beneath your wings, propelling you to heights you might have only dreamed of.

Key Takeaways

- Collaboration amplifies individual strengths, creating a dynamic synergy that drives success.

- Deep, transformative relationships enrich both your personal and professional lives.

- Mentors and allies provide invaluable guidance, wisdom, and support on your journey.

- Giving back is a powerful way to strengthen your support system and contribute to the success of others.

- Building a diverse and well-balanced support ecosystem is a strategic move toward achieving your full potential.

- Be open to feedback for continuous improvement.

- Leverage opportunities within your network for growth and success.

As we conclude this chapter on building and nurturing your support system, take a moment to assess your current support network. Who are the individuals and resources that have been instrumental in your journey so far? Identify any gaps or areas where you need to strengthen your support.

In the next chapter, we will delve deeper into unlocking the remarkable capabilities that reside within you. You will explore strategies to embrace your true potential, find your purpose, and set the course for a life of fulfillment and success. Get ready to discover the path to your own extraordinary potential!

Part 3: Thriving Beyond Self-Sabotage

Chapter 7: Embracing Your Full Potential

The story of Wilma Rudolph is one to behold when talking about embracing your full potential. Born prematurely and with a deformed foot, she was also diagnosed with polio at the age of four, which left her with a permanent limp. Doctors told her she would never walk.

But Wilma refused to give up. She worked hard with physical therapy and eventually learned to walk. She also started running and quickly became one of the fastest girls in her school.

In high school, Wilma Rudolph won the state championships in the 100-yard dash and the 200-yard dash. She also qualified for the Olympic trials, but she did not make the team.

Wilma was not discouraged. She continued to train and work hard. In 1960, she made the Olympic team and competed in the 100-meter dash, 200-meter dash, and 4x100-meter relay.

Wilma Rudolph won three gold medals at the 1960 Olympics, becoming the first American woman to win three gold medals in track and field. She was also the first African-American woman to win an Olympic gold medal in track and field.

Wilma Rudolph's story is an inspiration for us all. It shows us that we can achieve anything we set our minds to, no matter what our challenges are. If Wilma could overcome her physical challenges and become a world-class athlete, then we can overcome our challenges and achieve our dreams.

Wilma's story is also relatable to many people. Many of us have faced challenges in our lives. We may have been told that we couldn't do something, or we may have doubted ourselves. But Wilma's story shows us that we can overcome any challenge if we never give up.

Wilma's story also teaches us the importance of hard work, determination, and never giving up on our dreams. If Wilma could achieve her dreams, then we can achieve ours too.

In this chapter, we'll explore the process of identifying our strengths and how to leverage them for personal growth and success. Let's Begin!

Identifying Your Strengths

Do you know what you're really good at? What are your unique talents and abilities? These questions might seem simple, but they hold the key to unlocking your full potential.

Strengths are the things that we are good at. They are our natural talents and abilities. They are the unique qualities, talents, and abilities that make you, well, you. Understanding and harnessing them can be the key to unleashing your potential.

Our strengths can be physical, mental, emotional, or social.

- Physical strengths: These are our physical abilities, such as our capabilities, endurance, and flexibility. They can help us excel in sports, physical activities, and other areas where physical exertion is required.

- Mental strengths: These are our cognitive abilities, such as our intelligence, creativity, and problem-solving skills. They can help us succeed in academics, work, and other areas where mental acuity is required.

- Emotional strengths: These are our emotional abilities, such as our resilience, optimism, and empathy. They can help us cope with challenges, stay positive, and build strong relationships.

- Social strengths: These are our interpersonal abilities, such as our communication, teamwork, and leadership skills. They can help us connect with others, build relationships, and achieve common goals.

Many of us are so accustomed to our own abilities that we do not recognize them. You might be exceptionally organized, have a talent for calming others in stressful situations, or possess a remarkable aptitude for problem-solving. These strengths are like second nature to you, but they can be your most potent tools for success.

Start by taking stock of your life experiences. What tasks or activities come naturally to you? What do people consistently praise you for? These clues can lead you to your strengths. Sometimes, asking friends or colleagues for their opinions can provide valuable insights you might have missed.

Why is it important to identify our strengths?

- Set realistic goals. When we know what we are good at, we can set goals that are challenging but achievable.

- Make better decisions. When we know our strengths, we can make decisions that are aligned with our abilities.

- Be more successful. When we use our strengths, we are more likely to be successful in our work, relationships, and other areas of life.

- Feel more confident. When we know our strengths, we feel more confident in ourselves and our abilities.

- Enjoy life more. When we use our strengths, we are more likely to enjoy our work and our relationships.

Discovering Your Unique Talents

Strengths come in many forms. Some people are naturally gifted communicators, able to convey complex ideas with ease. Others have an artistic flair, an intuitive understanding of numbers, or an uncanny ability to connect with animals. Your strengths are like the colors on your personal palette, waiting for you to blend them into the masterpiece of your life.

Take some time for introspection. Reflect on the activities or tasks that bring you joy and fulfillment. When do you feel most 'in your element'? These moments often reveal your strengths in action.

Leveraging Strengths for Success

Identifying your strengths is not a mere task when it comes to self-awareness; it's a strategic move toward success. Your strengths are your superpowers, and they can be harnessed to achieve your goals. Imagine trying to build a house without the right tools; it would be a daunting task. Similarly, navigating life without leveraging your strengths can be needlessly challenging.

Suppose you're particularly skilled at problem-solving. In your career, you might gravitate toward roles that require creative solutions or analytical thinking. If you're an empathetic communicator, leadership positions that demand teamwork and collaboration could be your forte.

Also, don't forget to celebrate your success. Take time to celebrate your strengths and accomplishments. This will help you build your confidence and self-esteem.

Remember, the important thing is to identify your strengths and use them to your advantage. When you do this, you will be more successful and happier in all areas of your life.

Embracing Challenges as Opportunities

Many people see challenges as obstacles to be avoided. They try to avoid them, or they give up when they encounter them. However, challenges can also be seen as opportunities for growth and learning.

When we face challenges head-on, we are forced to step outside of our comfort zone and learn new things. We may also have to develop new skills and abilities. This can lead to personal growth and the realization of our potential.

Resilience is the key to embracing challenges as opportunities. It's the ability to bounce back from setbacks, to adapt, and to thrive in the face of adversity. Research has shown that resilience is not an inherent trait but a skill that can be cultivated. By developing resilience, you can transform challenges into stepping stones.

Here are some of the benefits of embracing challenges:

1. We Learn and Grow. When we face challenges, we are forced to learn new things and develop new skills. This can help us grow as individuals and become more well-rounded people.

2. We Become More Resilient. When we learn to overcome challenges, we become more resilient. This means that we are better able to cope with difficult situations and bounce back from setbacks.

3. We Become More Confident. When we achieve our goals, even in the face of challenges, we become more confident in our abilities. This can lead to greater success in all areas of our lives.

4. We Find Our Purpose. Sometimes, challenges can help us discover our purpose in life. When we find something that we are passionate about and that we are willing to work hard for, we can achieve great things.

Turning Adversity into Advantage

Nelson Mandela's life is a testament to the extraordinary power of resilience and the ability to turn profound challenges into opportunities for personal growth and societal change.

In 1962, Nelson Mandela was arrested and subsequently sentenced to life in prison for his involvement in anti-apartheid activities. For 27 long years, he endured the harsh conditions of Robben Island and other prisons. His confinement could have easily embittered him, extinguishing the flame of hope for reconciliation and justice.

However, Mandela chose a different path. During his time in prison, he transformed himself and his outlook on the world. He used his incarceration as an opportunity to learn, reflect, and educate both himself and his fellow inmates. Mandela and his fellow prisoners engaged in secret study groups where they discussed politics, philosophy, and history. This clandestine education became a vital source of inspiration and knowledge.

Mandela also recognized that the key to dismantling apartheid lay in forgiveness and reconciliation, not vengeance. He initiated talks with the apartheid government, even from his prison cell, to negotiate the end of apartheid and the transition to majority rule.

When Mandela was finally released in 1990, he emerged not as a bitter man seeking revenge but as a statesman committed to peace and reconciliation. His ability to forgive those who had oppressed him and to forge a new, democratic South Africa astounded the world.

In 1994, Nelson Mandela was elected as South Africa's first black president in the country's first democratic election. He had turned his imprisonment into a powerful tool for change, demonstrating that even the harshest challenges could be embraced as opportunities to learn, grow, and effect profound transformation.

Mandela's life serves as an enduring example of the human capacity to transcend adversity, maintain hope in the face of despair, and to use even the darkest moments as catalysts for personal and societal progress. His legacy is a beacon of resilience and an inspiration to all who face challenges in their pursuit of a better world.

Practical Steps to Embrace Challenges

1. Shift Your Perspective. When faced with a challenge, pause and reframe it as an opportunity for growth. Ask yourself what you can learn from this experience.

2. Set Realistic Goals. Break down larger challenges into smaller, manageable goals. Each achievement will boost your confidence and motivation.

3. Seek Support. Don't hesitate to lean on your support network—friends, family, mentors, or therapists—for guidance and encouragement.

4. Learn from Failure. Instead of dwelling on your mistakes, analyze them objectively. What went wrong, and what can you do differently next time?

5. Persist and Adapt. Persevere in the face of setbacks, but be willing to adapt your approach as needed. Flexibility is a valuable asset.

6. Celebrate Small Wins. Acknowledge and celebrate your achievements, no matter how small they may seem. These victories build momentum.

Embracing challenges as opportunities is a mindset that can profoundly impact your personal growth and help you realize your full potential. Remember that the most successful people often face the greatest challenges. As you navigate the ups and downs of life, keep in mind that each challenge is a chance for growth, learning, and, ultimately, transformation.

Overcoming Challenges

Everyone faces challenges in life. These challenges can be small, like a bad day at work, or they can be large, like a serious illness, the loss of a job, or the loss of a loved one.

How we deal with challenges is what matters. If we can learn to overcome challenges, we will be more resilient and better able to cope with whatever life throws our way.

Dealing with Challenges and Setbacks

Challenges come in various shapes and sizes—personal, professional, or the unexpected curveballs life throws our way. The first step in overcoming them is acknowledging their presence. Denial only prolongs the struggle. Allow yourself to feel your emotions, but don't dwell on them.

Acceptance, on the other hand, empowers you to take action.

The key is to approach challenges with a problem-solving mindset. Break them down into manageable steps, and look for the silver lining in every situation. Seek advice when needed, and remember that it's okay to ask for help. Don't just sit around and wait for the challenge to go away. Take steps to overcome it.

Developing a Growth Mindset

The notion of a growth mindset, popularized by psychologist Carol Dweck, is a powerful tool for overcoming challenges. It's the belief that your abilities and intelligence can be developed through dedication and hard work. When you cultivate a growth mindset, challenges become opportunities for growth rather than threats to your self-worth.

Start by reframing your self-talk. Instead of saying, "I can't do this," say, "I can't do this yet." Embrace the "yet" and open the door to growth.

Believe in Yourself

The most significant obstacle you'll ever face is often the one in the mirror. Self-doubt can be paralyzing, preventing you from realizing your potential. To overcome this, start by recognizing your achievements, no matter how small. Keep a journal of your successes, and when self-doubt creeps in, review it for a confidence boost.

Remember that believing in yourself isn't a solo journey. Seek out mentors, friends, or support groups that can reinforce your self-belief. Surrounding yourself with positive influences can make a world of difference.

Never Give Up on Your Dreams

Walt Disney, the man behind the world's most famous mouse, once said, "All our dreams can come true if we have the courage to pursue them." Your dreams are the compass guiding you toward your full potential. It's easy to lose sight of them amidst challenges, but they should be your North Star.

Perseverance is the key. Edison didn't invent the light bulb on the first try, and J.K. Rowling faced numerous rejections before Harry Potter found a home. Your journey might be tough, but it's your unique path to greatness. Keep pushing forward, and you'll be amazed at what you can achieve.

Challenges are not roadblocks to your potential; they are stepping stones.

Overcoming Limiting Beliefs

Limiting beliefs are like invisible chains that hold us back from reaching our full potential. They are the whispers of doubt that convince us we're not good enough, smart enough, or talented enough to achieve our dreams. But here's the truth: These beliefs are nothing more than stories we tell ourselves, and they can be rewritten.

Limiting beliefs often stem from past experiences, childhood conditioning, or societal influences. They take root in our minds and shape our thoughts, actions, and decisions. These beliefs can be paralyzing, keeping us stuck in our comfort zones and preventing us from taking risks or pursuing our passions.

How do limiting beliefs hinder personal growth?

Limiting beliefs can hinder personal growth in a number of ways. They can:

- Prevent us from taking risks. When we believe that we can't do something, we are less likely to try it. This can prevent us from learning and growing.

- Make us give up easily. When we believe that we're not good enough, we're more likely to give up when things get tough. This can prevent us from achieving our goals.

- Lead to self-sabotage. When we believe that we don't deserve success, we may sabotage our own efforts. This can prevent us from reaching our full potential.

How to overcome limiting beliefs

There are a number of strategies that can help us overcome limiting beliefs. Here are a few:

- Identify your limiting beliefs. The first step is to identify the limiting beliefs that are holding you back. What are the things that you tell yourself that you can't do?

- Challenge your beliefs. Once you have identified your limiting beliefs, challenge them. Ask yourself if there is any evidence to support these beliefs. Are they really true?

- Replace your beliefs with positive ones. Once you have challenged your limiting beliefs, replace them with positive ones. What would you like to believe about yourself?

- Take action. The best way to overcome limiting beliefs is to take action. When you take action, you are proving to yourself that you can do it. This will help you build your confidence and self-esteem.

- Seek help from a therapist or counselor. If you are struggling to overcome your limiting beliefs, you may want to seek help from a therapist or counselor. They can help you identify and challenge your beliefs and develop a plan for overcoming them.

Mindset shifts to help overcome limiting beliefs

Changing your mindset is a powerful tool for overcoming limiting beliefs. Consider adopting the following mindset shifts:

- From "I can't" to "I can learn": Replace the belief that you can't do something with the idea that you can learn and improve over time.

- From "I'm not good enough" to "I am worthy": Recognize your inherent worthiness and that mistakes and imperfections are part of being human.

- From "What if I fail?" to "What if I succeed?": Reframe your fear of failure as a fear of success. Ask yourself what opportunities and growth may come from succeeding.

Remember, limiting beliefs are just thoughts. They are not facts. You can choose to believe them or not. If you want to achieve your goals, it is important to challenge your limiting beliefs and adopt a positive mindset.

Living a Fulfilling Life

A fulfilling life is one that is meaningful and purposeful. It is a life that is lived in alignment with your values and goals. It is a life that is full of joy, satisfaction, and contentment.

How to live a fulfilling life

There are many things that you can do to live a fulfilling life. Here are a few:

- Find your passion. What are you passionate about? What makes you come alive? When you are passionate about something, you are more likely to be motivated and engaged.

- Pursue your goals. What are your goals in life? What do you want to achieve? When you have goals, you have something to strive for. This can give your life meaning and purpose.

- Help others. One of the best ways to find fulfillment in life is to help others. When you help others, you make a difference in the world and feel good about yourself.

- Be grateful. Take the time to appreciate the good things in your life. When you are grateful, you focus on the positive and feel happier.

- Live in the present moment. Don't dwell on the past or worry about the future. Focus on the present moment and enjoy it.

- Take care of yourself. Make sure to take care of your physical and mental health. When you are healthy, you have more energy and are better able to enjoy life.

- Spend time with loved ones. Make time for the people you love. They are the ones who will be there for you through thick and thin.

- Be kind to yourself. Be patient with yourself, and don't expect perfection. Everyone makes mistakes.

Finding your passion and pursuing it

Your passion is what you are good at and what you love to do. It is the thing that makes you come alive. When you are passionate about something, you are more likely to be motivated and engaged. You are also more likely to be successful.

Your passion is the fuel that ignites your potential. Think about the times when you've felt most alive and engaged. What were you doing? What activities brought you deep satisfaction and fulfillment? These are often clues to your passion. Embrace them and make them a more significant part of your life.

Purpose and Making a Difference

Living a fulfilling life goes hand in hand with having a sense of purpose. Purpose gives your life direction and deeper meaning. It's about understanding what you're uniquely positioned to contribute to the world.

There are many ways to make a difference in the world. Here are a few:

- Volunteer your time. There are many organizations that need volunteers. You can volunteer your time to help those in need.

- Donate to charity. There are many charities that are doing great work. You can donate money or other resources to help them.

- Advocate for a cause. If you are passionate about a cause, you can advocate for it. You can write letters to your elected officials, attend protests, or start a petition.

- Be a good role model. You can make a difference in the world by being a good role model. Be kind, compassionate, and helpful.

- Educate yourself. The more you know about the world, the better equipped you will be to make a difference.

No matter how big or small, every act of kindness makes a difference. So go out there and make a difference in the world!

As you embark on this journey, remember that fulfillment is a lifelong pursuit. It evolves as you grow and change. Embrace the challenges and joys along the way, for they are all part of the tapestry of a truly fulfilling life. Your potential is vast, and your life is the canvas—paint it with purpose, passion, and a commitment to making a difference.

Key Takeaways

- Self-discovery is a foundational step toward embracing your potential.

- Exploring your values, strengths, and passions can uncover hidden talents.

- Discovering your life's purpose can profoundly impact your personal growth.

- Purpose provides direction and a sense of fulfillment in life.

- Limiting beliefs hinder personal growth; challenge and replace them.

- Your mindset shapes your reality; cultivate a positive and growth-oriented mindset.

- A growth mindset fosters resilience and adaptability.

- Embrace challenges as opportunities for learning and growth.

- Facing challenges head-on can lead to profound personal development.

- Adversity can be a catalyst for realizing your untapped potential.

As we conclude this transformative chapter on embracing your full potential, it's time to put your newfound insights into action. Take some time to reflect on your values, strengths, and passions. Consider how they align with your current pursuits. Begin defining your life's purpose and setting meaningful goals that align with it. These goals will become your guiding stars, and the next time you face a challenge or setback, remind yourself that it's an opportunity for growth.

In the next chapter, you will learn practical strategies to turn your potential into a life filled with purpose, joy, and fulfillment.

Chapter 8: Navigating Relationships and Communication

I was in a meeting with my team, and we were discussing a new project. I was trying to explain my ideas, but I could tell that my team members were not understanding me. I tried to rephrase my ideas, but it was no use. We were just talking past each other.

Finally, I stopped and asked my team members if they had any questions. They all shook their heads. "I think we're just not on the same page," I said. "Can we take a break and come back to this later?"

We took a break, and I thought about what had gone wrong. I realized that I had been doing all the talking. I hadn't really listened to what my team members had to say. I had just assumed that they understood what I was saying, but they didn't.

When we came back to the meeting, I started by asking my team members what they thought about the project. I listened carefully to their ideas, and I asked questions to make sure I understood them. We talked back and forth until we all had a good understanding of the project.

The meeting went much better the second time around. We were able to come up with a plan that everyone was on board with. I learned a valuable lesson that day: communication is essential for building strong relationships.

We have all been in situations where we have tried to communicate with someone but have not been able to get our point across. It is important to listen to others and understand their point of view. When we communicate effectively, we are able to build stronger relationships and achieve our goals.

The Dynamics of Effective Communication

In the heart of every successful relationship, personal or professional, lies the bedrock of effective communication. It's not just about talking; it's about connecting, understanding, and being understood.

Verbal Communication: The Power of Words

Think about the last time someone's words made your day or utterly ruined it. Words possess immense power, and the way we use them can shape our relationships and our lives. Effective verbal communication involves not just what we say but also how we say it.

- Tone: It's not just about what you say but also how you say it. Tone can convey empathy or indifference, enthusiasm or apathy. We'll explore the importance of tone and how it can be a game-changer in your interactions.

- Clarity: Have you ever received an email or a message that left you scratching your head, trying to decipher its meaning? Clarity in communication is like a breath of fresh air. We'll delve into techniques to make your communication crystal clear and easily understood.

- Choice of Words: Words can build bridges or create chasms. The words you choose can make all the difference. We'll discuss strategies for selecting the right words in various contexts to convey your thoughts effectively.

Nonverbal Communication: Beyond Words

Ever heard the phrase, "Actions speak louder than words"? Nonverbal communication is like the silent orchestra accompanying our spoken words. It includes body language, facial expressions, and gestures that can amplify or contradict what we say verbally.

- Body Language: Your posture, gestures, and body movements communicate volumes. We'll explore the art of using body language to enhance your message and foster better connections.

- Facial Expressions: The face is a canvas of emotions. We'll decode the subtle and not-so-subtle cues that your face can reveal and how to use them to your advantage.

- Gestures: From a friendly wave to a firm handshake, gestures are a universal language. We'll discuss how gestures can convey trust, confidence, and sincerity in your interactions.

Active Listening: The Art of Truly Hearing

In a world full of noise, active listening is a rare gem. It's not just about hearing words; it's about understanding the emotions, intentions, and unspoken messages behind them.

- The Importance of Listening: We'll emphasize the significance of active listening in building meaningful relationships and how it can lead to better collaboration and problem-solving.

- Empathetic Listening: Understanding someone's perspective and showing empathy can transform a conversation. We'll provide practical tips for becoming a more empathetic listener.

- Responding Thoughtfully: Active listening is not complete without thoughtful responses. We'll explore techniques for responding in a way that validates the speaker and fosters constructive dialogue.

These skills are not just about conveying information; they're about creating connections and understanding others on a deeper level.

Navigating Conflict and Difficult Conversations

Conflict is a natural part of life. It can happen in our personal and professional lives; conflicts are inevitable. Whether it's a disagreement with a colleague, a dispute with a family member, or a tense discussion with a friend, conflict can create tension and discomfort. However, it's essential to understand that conflict itself is not inherently negative. In fact, when managed effectively, conflicts can lead to growth, improved relationships, and innovative solutions.

Conflict Resolution Strategies

The key to turning conflicts into opportunities lies in employing effective conflict resolution strategies. Here are some proven methods to help you resolve conflicts constructively:

1. Active Listening. The foundation of conflict resolution is active listening. When engaged in a conflict, make a conscious effort to truly hear what the other person is saying without interrupting or formulating your response. This demonstrates respect and allows the other person to feel heard and understood.

2. Empathy. Empathy is the ability to understand and share the feelings of another. Put yourself in the other person's shoes and try to see the situation from their perspective. This can be a powerful tool for defusing conflicts, as it shows that you genuinely care about their feelings.

3. Open Communication. Encourage open and honest communication. Express your own thoughts and feelings clearly and respectfully, and encourage the other party to do the same. Sometimes, conflicts arise from misunderstandings that can be cleared up through effective communication.

4. Problem-Solving. Approach conflicts as problems to be solved together. Instead of viewing the other person as an adversary, work collaboratively to find solutions that benefit both parties. This shift in mindset can transform a conflict into a constructive dialogue.

Difficult Conversations

Difficult conversations are a subset of conflicts that involve sensitive or uncomfortable topics. Handling them with empathy and care is crucial. Here's how to navigate these discussions effectively:

1. Prepare Ahead. Before engaging in a difficult conversation, take time to prepare. Clarify your goals and intentions for the conversation. Think about what you want to communicate and how you want the other person to feel afterward.

2. Choose the Right Time and Place. Timing and location matter. Select a time and place where both you and the other party can focus on the conversation without distractions or time constraints.

3. Use "I" Statements. When expressing your feelings or concerns, use "I" statements to avoid sounding accusatory. For example, say, "I felt hurt when..." instead of "You hurt me when..."

4. Stay Calm. Emotional regulation is essential. If emotions start to run high, take a break if needed. Returning to the conversation with a clear mind and controlled emotions can prevent escalation.

Emotional Regulation

Emotional regulation is a fundamental skill for handling conflicts and difficult conversations. Here are some techniques to help you manage your emotions during challenging interactions:

- Deep Breathing: When you feel emotions intensifying, pause and take several deep breaths. This simple technique can help calm your nervous system and reduce emotional reactivity.

- Mindfulness: Practicing mindfulness can enhance emotional regulation. It involves being fully present in the moment and observing your thoughts and feelings without judgment. This awareness can help you choose how to respond rather than react impulsively.

- Self-Care: Ensure you are taking care of your physical and emotional well-being outside of the conflict. A healthy lifestyle, including regular exercise, adequate sleep, and stress reduction techniques, can equip you to handle conflicts more effectively.

Navigating conflict and difficult conversations can be challenging, but it is an essential skill for building strong relationships and achieving our goals. By understanding the different conflict resolution strategies and how to handle difficult conversations, we can learn to manage conflict in a constructive way.

Building and Maintaining Professional Networks

In today's interconnected world, the power of networking cannot be overstated. It's not just about collecting business cards or connecting on LinkedIn; it's about forging meaningful relationships that can propel your personal and professional growth.

Networking

At its core, networking is about creating mutually beneficial relationships. It's not solely reserved for white-collar jobs or salespeople; it's for anyone looking to grow, learn, and succeed.

Networking isn't just about what you can gain; it's also about what you can give. The most effective networkers approach interactions with a mindset of offering help, support, and knowledge. It's a two-way street where both parties benefit.

Research has shown that networking can lead to new opportunities, job offers, and career advancement. But it's essential to remember that building a valuable network takes time and sincerity.

Strategic Networking

While casual connections are valuable, strategic networking involves identifying and connecting with individuals who can specifically help you reach your career goals. Start by defining your objectives - what do you hope to achieve through networking?

Consider joining professional organizations, attending conferences, or participating in online forums relevant to your industry. These platforms can provide opportunities to connect with like-minded individuals and industry leaders.

It's also important to be genuine in your interactions. Authenticity goes a long way toward building trust. Remember that networking isn't just about the quantity of connections; the quality of those connections matters more.

Maintaining Relationships

Building a network is just the beginning; maintaining it is equally crucial. Think of your network as a garden - it requires care and attention to flourish.

Stay in touch with your contacts regularly. Send emails, make phone calls, or meet for coffee. Share useful information, congratulate them on their achievements, and offer your support when needed.

Additionally, leverage social media platforms to stay connected. LinkedIn, for instance, can be a powerful tool for nurturing and expanding your professional network.

Remember that relationships are built on trust, so be reliable and helpful. When you offer your assistance without expecting immediate returns, you strengthen your network's bonds.

Building and maintaining professional networks is not a one-time effort; it's an ongoing process that evolves with your career. As you invest time and effort into nurturing these relationships, you'll find that your network becomes a valuable asset, opening doors to opportunities you might never have imagined.

Leading with Emotional Intelligence

Emotional intelligence, often referred to as EQ (Emotional Quotient), has emerged as a critical skill in the contemporary world, influencing our interactions, relationships, and leadership capacities. In this section, we'll delve into the essence of leading with emotional intelligence, exploring its three fundamental pillars: emotional awareness, empathy, and emotionally intelligent leadership.

Emotional Awareness

Imagine you're in the midst of a high-stakes business negotiation, and tension fills the room. You notice your heart racing, your palms becoming clammy, and a rising sense of frustration. These are your emotional cues, signaling your inner state.

Emotional awareness is the cornerstone of emotional intelligence. It involves the ability to recognize and understand your own emotions as they arise. This self-awareness enables you to navigate situations with greater clarity and composure.

Practical Steps for Enhancing Emotional Awareness:

- Mindfulness Practices: Engage in mindfulness meditation or breathing exercises to connect with your emotional state.

- Journaling: Maintain a journal to record your daily emotional experiences and reflections.

- Feedback Seeking: Encourage honest feedback from trusted peers or mentors to gain insights into your emotional responses.

Empathy

Empathy is the capacity to step into someone else's shoes and understand their feelings, perspectives, and needs. It's the bridge that connects individuals and fosters deep, meaningful relationships. Empathetic leaders have an innate ability to create inclusive, supportive environments.

Imagine a manager who listens intently to her team members' concerns, not just hearing their words but sensing their emotions. This empathetic approach builds trust and collaboration, creating a harmonious workplace.

Practical Steps for Cultivating Empathy

- Active Listening: Practice attentive, nonjudgmental listening when engaging with others.

- Perspective-Taking: Make an effort to see situations from different viewpoints.

- Empathy Exercises: Engage in empathy-building exercises, such as reflecting on others' emotions and experiences.

Emotionally Intelligent Leadership

Leadership in the modern era extends far beyond technical skills and expertise. Emotionally intelligent leadership involves leveraging emotional awareness and empathy to guide teams effectively. It's about recognizing that people are not just resources but individuals with emotions, aspirations, and potential.

Imagine a CEO who understands the anxieties of employees during times of change and communicates with empathy and transparency. This fosters a culture of trust and adaptability, propelling the organization forward.

Practical Steps for Emotionally Intelligent Leadership

- Conflict Resolution: Develop strategies for addressing conflicts while considering the emotions of all parties involved.

- Team Building: Foster a supportive team environment by acknowledging and valuing each team member's contributions.

- Feedback Delivery: Provide constructive feedback with sensitivity, focusing on growth and development.

Incorporating emotional intelligence into your leadership approach can transform your professional interactions and create a more positive and productive environment. As you harness the power of emotional awareness, empathy, and emotionally intelligent leadership, you'll find that you not only lead with confidence but also inspire others to excel.

Cultivating a Global Perspective

In today's world, the ability to navigate diverse cultures and engage effectively with people from various backgrounds is a skill of paramount importance. Cultivating a global perspective is more than just knowing about different countries or being able to greet people in multiple languages. It's about developing a mindset that embraces diversity, values inclusivity, and seeks to understand the intricate tapestry of our world.

Global Awareness

Imagine being at ease in conversations with people from all corners of the globe, not because you've traveled extensively but because you possess global awareness. This awareness is about recognizing the rich diversity of cultures, traditions, and worldviews that shape our planet. It's acknowledging that there isn't a one-size-fits-all approach to life, and that's what makes our world fascinating.

Global awareness begins with curiosity. It's about seeking to understand the customs, beliefs, and values of different societies. It's realizing that while your way of life might be perfectly suitable for you, it might not apply universally. It's also about being aware of global issues, from climate change to social justice, and recognizing how they impact different regions.

To cultivate global awareness, start by engaging with people from different backgrounds. Listen to their stories, learn about their experiences, and ask questions. Read about world events, follow international news, and explore documentaries and literature from various cultures. It's not about becoming an expert in every culture but rather appreciating and respecting the diversity that enriches our world.

Cross-Cultural Communication

Effective cross-cultural communication is the bridge that connects people from different backgrounds. It's more than just words; it's the ability to convey ideas, emotions, and intentions across cultural boundaries. It's about ensuring that your message is not only heard but also understood in the way you intended.

One essential aspect of cross-cultural communication is sensitivity. This means being aware of cultural differences in communication styles, body language, and social norms. What may be a polite gesture in one culture could be considered rude in another. Learning these nuances can help you navigate conversations respectfully.

Active listening is another key element. It involves not only hearing words but also understanding the context and emotions behind them. Ask for clarification if needed, and show empathy toward different viewpoints. Effective communication often involves asking open-ended questions, allowing others to share their perspectives more deeply.

Building cross-cultural communication skills takes time and practice. Don't be discouraged by occasional misunderstandings; they are opportunities for growth. As you engage in conversations with people from diverse backgrounds, you'll become more adept at bridging cultural gaps and fostering connections.

Being a Global Citizen

Becoming a global citizen goes beyond having a passport. It's about recognizing your role in a world that's increasingly interconnected. Global citizenship means taking responsibility for the planet and its inhabitants, regardless of borders.

One hallmark of global citizenship is active engagement in global issues. It's understanding that challenges like climate change, poverty, and human rights violations affect us all, no matter where we live. It's advocating for positive change and supporting initiatives that contribute to a better world.

Global citizenship also involves ethical consumption and responsible travel. It's about making choices that minimize harm to the environment and respecting the cultures and communities you encounter. It's being aware of your carbon footprint and making efforts to reduce it.

In conclusion, cultivating a global perspective is not just a skill; it's a mindset. It's about recognizing the beauty in our world's diversity, communicating effectively across cultures, and taking responsibility as a global citizen. By embracing these principles, you not only enrich your own life but also contribute to the collective well-being of our interconnected world.

Key Takeaways

- Verbal communication involves tone, clarity, and word choice.

- Nonverbal communication includes body language, facial expressions, and gestures.

- Active listening is crucial for understanding and building connections.

- Conflict is a natural part of relationships, but it can be managed constructively.

- Effective communication techniques, such as empathy and compromise, can resolve conflicts.

- Difficult conversations require preparation, a calm demeanor, and a focus on solutions.

- Networking is a powerful tool for personal and career growth.

- Building relationships should be genuine, based on mutual interests and trust.

- Maintaining networks involves regular communication and providing value.

- Emotional intelligence enhances leadership by fostering self-awareness, empathy, and effective communication.

In this chapter, we've explored the multifaceted dynamics of effective communication, discovered how to navigate conflicts and difficult conversations, learned the art of building and maintaining professional networks, dived into the realm of leading with emotional intelligence, and cultivated a global perspective.

Take some time to evaluate your communication style. Are there areas where you could improve, such as active listening or clarifying your messages?

Invest in your emotional intelligence. Explore books, courses, or coaching that can help you enhance your self-awareness, empathy, and emotional regulation skills.

Conclusion

Putting It All Together: A Plan for Lasting Change

I'm happy that you made it to the end of this book. You have now learned a lot about self-sabotage and how to overcome it. You have learned how to identify your self-sabotaging behaviors, understand the root causes of self-sabotage, disrupt negative thought patterns and beliefs, cultivate positive habits and behaviors, build resilience and self-compassion, create a support system for success, and embrace your full potential.

Now, it is time to put all of this knowledge into practice. Here is a detailed plan for lasting change:

1. Start by setting some goals. What do you want to achieve in your life? Once you know what you want, you can start to make a plan for how to get there. Your goals should be specific, measurable, achievable, relevant, and time-bound. For example, you might set a goal to lose 10 pounds in 3 months or to get a promotion at work within a year.

- Specific: Your goals should be specific enough that you can measure your progress. For example, instead of saying,

"I want to lose weight, say, "I want to lose 10 pounds in 3 months."

- Measurable: Your goals should be measurable so that you can track your progress. For example, instead of saying, "I want to be more confident, say, "I want to give a presentation at work without feeling nervous."

- Achievable: Your goals should be achievable but challenging. If your goals are too easy, you won't be motivated to achieve them. If your goals are too difficult, you'll be discouraged and give up.

- Relevant: Your goals should be relevant to your values and priorities. If your goals are not relevant to what you care about, you're less likely to stick with them.

- Time-bound: Your goals should have a specific deadline. This will help you stay focused and motivated.

2. Identify your self-sabotaging behaviors. What are the things that you do that hold you back from achieving your goals? Once you know what these behaviors are, you can start to work on changing them. Common self-sabotaging behaviors include procrastination, perfectionism, and negative self-talk.

- Procrastination: Procrastination is the act of delaying or postponing a task or set of tasks. It can be a major obstacle to achieving your goals. To overcome procrastination, try breaking down your goals into smaller, more manageable steps. And then set a deadline for each step.

- Perfectionism: Perfectionism is the pursuit of flawlessness. It can be a major obstacle to achieving your goals because it can lead to procrastination, anxiety, and stress. To overcome perfectionism, try to focus on progress instead of perfection. And remember, it's okay to make mistakes.

- Negative self-talk: Negative self-talk is the way we talk to ourselves about ourselves. It can be very destructive and hold us back from achieving our goals. To overcome negative self-talk, try to be more mindful of your thoughts. And when you catch yourself thinking negative thoughts, challenge them.

3. Challenge your negative thoughts. When you have negative thoughts about yourself or your ability to succeed, challenge them. Ask yourself if they are really true. For example, if you think, "I'm not smart enough to get that promotion," ask yourself why you believe that. Are there any facts to support your belief? Or is it just a story you're telling yourself?

- Reframe your negative thoughts: Once you've challenged your negative thoughts, try to reframe them in a more positive way. For example, instead of saying, "I'm not smart enough to get that promotion, say, "I'm going to do everything I can to get that promotion."

- Practice positive self-talk. Positive self-talk is the opposite of negative self-talk. It's the way we talk to ourselves in a positive and supportive way. To practice positive self-talk, try to focus on your strengths and accomplishments. And when you make a mistake, don't beat yourself up about it. Just learn from it and move on.

5. Take care of yourself. Make sure that you are getting enough sleep, eating healthy foods, and exercising regularly. This will help you have the energy and focus you need to succeed. When you take care of yourself, you're better able to handle stress and resist temptation.

- Get enough sleep: When you're well-rested, you're better able to focus and make good decisions. Aim for 7-8 hours of sleep per night.

- Eat healthy foods: Eating healthy foods will give you the energy you need to power through your day. Choose foods that are high in nutrients and low in processed sugar and unhealthy fats.

- Exercise regularly: Exercise is a great way to reduce stress, improve your mood, and boost your energy levels. Aim for at least 30 minutes of moderate-intensity exercise most days of the week.

6. Find a support system. Surround yourself with people who believe in you and support your goals. This could include friends, family, a therapist, or a coach. Having a support system will help you stay accountable and motivated.

- Talk to your friends and family: Let your loved ones know about your goals and ask for their support. They can help you stay on track and celebrate your successes.

- Seek professional help: If you're struggling to overcome self-sabotage, consider talking to a therapist or coach. They can help you identify the root causes of your self-sabotage and develop strategies for overcoming it.

7. Don't give up. Change takes time and effort. Don't give up if you don't see results immediately. Just keep moving forward, and you will eventually achieve your goals. Remember, everyone experiences setbacks along the way. The important thing is to keep learning and growing from your mistakes.

- Start taking action today. Don't wait for the perfect moment to start making changes. Just start where you are and keep moving forward.

- Be patient and persistent. Change takes time and effort. Don't get discouraged if you don't see results immediately. Just keep going, and you will eventually reach your goals.

- Don't give up on yourself. You are capable of achieving anything you set your mind to. Believe in yourself, and never give up on your dreams.

Today, you stand at the precipice of transformation. The choice is yours: to step back into the shadows of old habits or to leap into the light of your full potential. Choose the latter. Take the wisdom you've gained, the insights you've uncovered, and the skills you've honed, and use them to build the life you envision.

- Begin Today: Transformation doesn't wait for tomorrow. Your first step is the most important. Take it now.

- Reflect and Adapt: Regularly review your progress. Celebrate your wins, learn from your setbacks, and adapt as needed.

- Pay It Forward: Share your journey with others. Your story can inspire and empower those around you.

- Embrace Uniqueness: Your path to success is unlike anyone else's. Embrace its uniqueness and trust your journey.

- Remember Your Why: In moments of doubt, revisit your intentions and the future you've envisioned. Let them fuel your determination.

Key Takeaways

- Self-Awareness is the First step. Understanding your own behaviors, motivations, and patterns is the foundation of personal growth.

- Break the Chains of Self-Sabotage. Recognize self-sabotaging behaviors and thought patterns and take action to overcome them.

- Root Causes Run Deep. Dive into your past and explore the origins of self-sabotage, allowing for deep healing and transformation.

- Empower Your Mind. Disrupt negative thought patterns and beliefs, replacing them with empowering and positive ones.

- Habits Shape Your Destiny. Cultivate positive habits and behaviors to create lasting change in your life.

- Resilience is Your armor. Learn to bounce back from setbacks, using failure as a stepping stone towards success.

- Support is Essential. Build a support system of like-minded individuals who uplift and encourage your journey.

- Unleash Your Full Potential. Embrace your unique talents and passions, and strive to fulfill your highest potential.

- Effective Communication is key. Master the art of communication to foster better relationships and understanding.

- Global Perspective, Local Impact Cultivate a global mindset, recognizing that your actions can create positive change on a larger scale.

These takeaways encapsulate the transformative journey you've embarked on, providing the keys to unlocking your full potential and living a fulfilling, self-sabotage-free life. Remember, lasting change is a journey, and by internalizing these lessons, you're equipped to navigate it successfully.

This book, "Breaking the Cycle of Self-Sabotage for Men," has equipped you with essential tools and insights to create a support system for success and embrace your full potential.

As we conclude this transformative journey together, remember that the story of your life is an ever-evolving masterpiece.

I believe in you! You have the power to overcome self-sabotage and build a fulfilling life.

I hope this book has been helpful to you. If you have any questions or need support, please feel free to reach out to me. I am here to help you on your journey to a fulfilling life.

If you enjoyed the book and found value in its content, please consider leaving a review on Amazon. Your feedback will not only inspire others to embark on their transformative journeys but also motivate us to continue creating meaningful content that empowers and uplifts.

THANK YOU

Thank you for choosing "Breaking the Cycle of Self-Sabotage for Men." Your support and interest in this book mean the world to me.

I poured my heart and soul into crafting this guide to provide expert insights and practical strategies to help you uncover your authentic self and achieve personal growth. I hope that you have found the content valuable and empowering.

As an independent author, your feedback and review on the platform where you purchased the book would be immensely valuable. By sharing your thoughts, you help me grow as a writer and also assist others in discovering the transformative power of embracing authenticity and purpose in their lives.

Your review can inspire and guide individuals seeking to overcome obstacles, find meaning in their journey, and live a fulfilling life aligned with their values. Your support fuels my passion for writing and motivates me to continue creating content that resonates with you and addresses your needs.

To leave a review please click below

Richard Garraway Author Page

Thank you for investing in "Breaking the Cycle of Self-Sabotage for Men." Let's create a world where individuals find their true selves, embrace their uniqueness, and achieve lasting personal fulfilment.

With heartfelt appreciation,

Richard Garraway

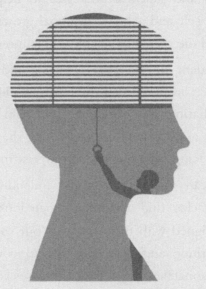

EMOTIONAL VULNERABILITY IN MEN

FINDING STRENGTH IN SENSITIVITY TO NAVIGATE RELATIONSHIPS, WORK, FATHERHOOD, AND MODERN MASCULINITY

RICHARD GARRAWAY

YOUR FREE GIFT

As a special thank you, I'm delighted to offer you a free gift
Introducing **"Your Emotional Intelligence Quiz"**

To claim your free gift and embark on this life-changing journey, visit:

https://richardgarrawaybooks.com/Free-Gift-7

Why take the quiz?

Gain Self-Awareness: Identify emotional strengths and growth areas to improve relationships, and communication.

Discover Your Emotional Intelligence Level: *Level 1: Exploring Emotional Awareness,* **Level 2:** *Embracing Emotional Growth,* **Level 3:** *Cultivating Emotional Balance,* **Level 4:** *Mastering Emotional Intelligence,* **Level 5:** *Elevating Emotional Mastery*

Personalized Guidance: Get custom feedback and actionable steps to boost emotional intelligence and personal growth.

Empowerment: Start enhancing your emotional skills for resilience and grace.

Direction: Set clear goals for improved emotional intelligence, leading to greater life fulfillment

Thank you for your support and trust in "Emotional Vulnerability in Men."

Richard Garraway.

Introduction

My son, barely eight years old, sat beside me, tears welling in his eyes. It was sports day at his elementary school. My son was in the baseball competition. I had seen him practice over the past few weeks, and he had been so excited about it, so I decided to be there to encourage him. His little face would light up. He swung the plastic bat, imagining hitting home runs like one of his favourite players.

The other kids lined up on the makeshift field. Their sneakers scuffed the grass. My son stood there, clutching the bat. He was so determined to win the game for his team.

His uniform was slightly too big for him, the cap slipping down over his eyes. But he didn't care; he was ready to give it his all.

As the game progressed, it became evident that victory wasn't on the cards for him. Despite his best efforts, the opposing team seemed to outshine him at every turn. The ball flew through the air, and my heart raced alongside it. I watched as my son swung, his small frame twisting with effort. But the ball sailed past him, and the disappointment in his eyes was palpable.

Then it happened—the final pitch, the decisive moment that sealed his team's loss.

As he left the pitch and walked to me, I felt pressure to be the "strong dad." I should offer a stoic pat on the back and a quick "good game." But this time, something felt different. As he reached the dugout, I kneeled, meeting his tear-filled eyes.

"Hey, champ," I said, my voice thick with emotion. "That was a tough game. You fought hard out there."

He sniffled, surprise flickering across his face. "We lost," he mumbled, kicking at a clump of dirt.

I smiled, a genuine one that warmed my own heart. "Yeah, we did. But you know what? Sometimes even the best teams lose."

His eyes widened as I continued, "The real win is how you played the game. Did you give it your all? Did you have fun?"

He hesitated for a moment, then a small smile tugged at the corners of his lips. "Yeah, I guess."

"That's what matters," I said, pulling him into a hug.

The warmth of his small body pressed against mine. At that moment, I realized my true strength. It wasn't about stoicism. It was about vulnerability. It was about acknowledging emotions. And, it was about creating a safe space for your child to do the same. He needed a hug. He also needed a word of encouragement and a shared moment of vulnerability. These things were more important than the outcome of the game. Taking a deep breath, I reached out and pulled my son into a tight embrace. "That's okay, champ," I whispered, my voice thick with emotion. "We'll practice together this week.

The rest of the day unfolded with cheers and laughter. We watched other games, shared snacks, and even got our faces painted with team colors.

The story you just read exemplifies the internal struggle men face.

Vulnerability isn't weakness; it is our bridge to authenticity. Maybe we could embrace it. Then, we could rewrite the rules of masculinity. We could create a world where tears show resilience, not defeat.

In the past, masculinity has meant stoicism and strength. Men have been conditioned to believe that vulnerability is weakness, a chink in our armour that exposes us to ridicule and rejection. But the reality is far more complex.

The modern landscape for men is a shifting one. Societal expectations are changing slowly. But the pressure to conform to old ideas of masculinity remains. We juggle careers, relationships, and families, all while navigating a constant double bind. Be strong and stoic, and be the rock. But also, be emotionally available, be a supportive partner, and be a present father. These seemingly contradictory expectations can leave us feeling isolated and confused.

Many men experience a constant internal battle. We want to connect with our loved ones and express our emotions openly, but the fear of judgment holds us back. We bottle up our feelings. This leads to emotional detachment and a disconnect from ourselves and those around us. This hidden struggle manifests in various ways – difficulty expressing anger or sadness, emotional withdrawal in relationships, and even struggles with mental health.

Vulnerability is not a flaw to be hidden, but a strength to be embraced.

In "Emotional Vulnerability in Men", we will break these walls and forge a path towards a more fulfilling life. Here, we'll tackle the complexities of emotional vulnerability head-on. We'll explore the concepts behind emotions, debunking the myth that expressing them diminishes our masculinity. We need to shift from the dynamics of societal expectations to dissecting traditional norms and exploring their impact on our emotional well-being in the modern world.

This is more than just a book; it's an invitation. An invitation to embark on a progressive journey of self-discovery. You will learn strategies for navigating difficult conversations. They will help you connect better with your partner and children. You will also learn to express your emotional needs in a healthy manner. This will help you become stronger.

This book stands as a beacon of guidance and empowerment. **As you read this book, it will help you:**

1. Understand the complexities of emotional vulnerability in men and how societal norms impact our ability to express and navigate our emotions authentically.

2. Recognize the hidden struggles you may face when navigating emotional expression, and provide you with tools to overcome these obstacles.

3. Embrace your full emotional spectrum by discovering how to acknowledge and express all your emotions, from joy and love to anger and sadness, healthily and authentically.

4. Challenge the pervasive societal norms and expectations that pressure men to conform to stoic expressions of strength and empower you to embrace vulnerability as a source of authenticity and resilience.

5. Building stronger relationships with the power of vulnerability to cultivate deeper connections with friends, family, and partners.

6. Thrive in the workplace by cultivating emotional intelligence, resilience, authenticity, and breaking free from the constraints of traditional masculinity.

7. Embrace fatherhood and parenting with empathy, understanding, and emotional openness, creating a nurturing and supportive environment for your children to flourish.

8. Cultivate a sense of community and connection with like-minded individuals who are also on a journey of self-discovery and authenticity.

9. Create a personal growth blueprint tailored to your unique journey, empowering you to live a more fulfilling and authentic life.

10. Creating a more fulfilling life by discovering the power of emotional vulnerability to build a life that is richer, more meaningful, and filled with deeper connections

I am not just the author of this book. I bring expertise in navigating vulnerability. I also understand the challenges men face. Together, we can find ourselves. We can learn the strategies to emerge stronger, more real, and truly empowered. I am also on this journey with you. I've been able to break this barrier, and I understand your struggles and believe unequivocally in your ability to overcome them.

Perhaps you're wondering, "Who am I to guide you on this journey?" As the author of this book, I've spent years exploring the complexities of masculinity and emotional vulnerability. I have seen the power of embracing our true selves. I saw it through my experience and research. My goal is to be your trusted companion on this path, offering insights, support, and the tools you need to thrive.

By the time you turn the final page, you won't just understand the challenges of emotional vulnerability in men; you'll be equipped to navigate them.

I am an individual with an unwavering passion for empowering men on their journey toward emotional vulnerability. I was fueled by a deep commitment. I wanted to break down societal norms and foster authenticity. I channeled this passion into writing this book.

Each person's journey is unique. This book gives tailored guidance, not generic advice. You will learn from a mix of psychology, exercises, and stories. The tools are made for your challenges.

Are you ready to accept your vulnerability? Doing so unlocks the power to build deeper connections and gain self-awareness. It also lets you forge a path to a richer life of purpose and fulfilment. It's time to embrace our emotions, share our stories, and rewrite the rules of masculinity. Turn the page and embark on a journey of emotional liberation. It's time to break the barriers.

Part 1: Unmasking Emotions - Recognizing and Embracing Vulnerability in Relationships

Chapter 1: The Hidden Struggle

Is vulnerability the same as weakness? We often link vulnerability with emotions we do not want to feel, like fear, shame, and uncertainty. However, we overlook that vulnerability is also where joy, creativity, authenticity, and love originate.

Our society has woven men into a rigid pattern of

stoicism, toughness, and emotional restraint. From a young age, a boy is taught to suppress his emotions and bury his vulnerabilities beneath his strength; if not, he will be seen as weak. Gradually, a hidden struggle, an internal conflict that festers in the shadows of masculinity, begins to surface.

Society often tells men to "man up" and bottle up their feelings. But emotions are a natural part of life, and pushing them down can be harmful. It can lead to feeling isolated, disconnected from loved ones, and even struggling with mental health.

Vulnerability isn't weakness. It's a strength. It takes courage to open up about what you're feeling, and it can lead to deeper connections with others. Being able to truly share your joys and sorrows with the people you care about is the power of emotional vulnerability.

This chapter delves into the invisible war men wage within themselves. In our exploration, we'll focus on the societal expectations that dictate traditional masculinity, highlighting the pressure to suppress emotions and maintain invulnerability. We'll look at the role of the media. We'll also look at family dynamics and cultural backgrounds. They shape these expectations. We'll also explore the psychological effects of emotional suppression. We'll look at the fear of judgment and the inner conflict. This conflict arises from wanting authenticity while fearing rejection. I will show you practical examples. You will learn to admit and handle these hidden struggles. This will pave the way for a journey of self-discovery and openness.

Societal Expectation

Societal expectations often cast men as the embodiment of traditional masculinity. Society has long prescribed a narrow definition of masculinity. It's like a script that dictates how men should behave, think, and, above all, feel. Many see stoicism, toughness, and restraint as the cornerstones of being a "real man."" But where did this script come from, and how is it affecting men today?

Traditional Masculinity

The pressure to conform to traditional ideas of masculinity can harm men's mental health and emotions.

Psychologists have long argued that suppressing emotions is not healthy. Studies by James Gross of Stanford University show that hiding emotions causes more stress. It also causes anxiety and health problems. Imagine a pressure cooker; the longer you keep the heat on without releasing the steam, the more likely it is to explode. The same principle applies to our emotions. When we don't healthily express them, they can build up and eventually erupt in unhealthy ways, like anger outbursts or withdrawal.

Media Influence

The media plays a significant role in shaping societal expectations of masculinity. Men are often shown this way in media, from movies to ads. These representations reinforce the idea that vulnerability is a sign of weakness, perpetuating harmful stereotypes and making it difficult for men to express their emotions openly.

A study published in the journal Sex Roles revealed that exposure to traditional masculine media messages is indeed associated with negative attitudes toward seeking help for mental health issues among men. The research highlights how adherence to masculine norms can impact men's mental health and their willingness to seek psychological assistance. It's essential to recognize and address these societal influences to promote better mental well-being for everyone.

These media portrayals reinforce the notion that vulnerability is a sign of weakness. The message is clear: real men don't cry, they conquer.

Research by the American Psychological Association (APA) suggests that men experience a full range of emotions, just like women. The difference lies not in the feeling itself but in how we're conditioned to express it.

Family and Cultural Upbringing

Family dynamics and cultural backgrounds also play a significant role in shaping men's attitudes toward emotional expression. In many households, boys are socialized to conform to traditional gender roles, with girls encouraged to be nurturing and emotional while boys are taught to be strong and stoic. This can create a sense of pressure for boys to suppress their emotions and conform to societal expectations of masculinity.

Cultural norms and traditions can further reinforce these expectations, making it challenging for men to break free from traditional gender roles. In some cultures, showing vulnerability or expressing emotions openly is seen as a sign of weakness, leading men to internalize these beliefs and hide their true feelings from others.

In conclusion, societal expectations of masculinity place a heavy burden on men, forcing them to conform to narrow ideals of strength and toughness while suppressing their emotions. This pressure to succumb to traditional norms can have negative consequences for men's mental and emotional well-being, contributing to feelings of isolation, loneliness, and emotional distress.

Unraveling the Emotional Suppression

Suppressing emotions may seem like a coping mechanism, but the psychological effect it has on men is profound.

Psychological Impact

Burying feelings can cause stress, anxiety, and depression. Suppressing emotions doesn't make them disappear. Instead, they fester, causing mental health issues.

Consider holding up a bottle of water; it feels weightless and effortless to hold. Imagine keeping it raised for a minute. Now, picture holding it for an entire hour. Over time, that weightless bottle would become unbearable. You might experience pain and even lose feeling in your arm. This reflects the impact of suppressing emotions. At first, it might seem inconsequential.

Continuing to bottle up feelings over time causes emotional weight to accumulate. This turns a small burden into a source of pain.

Numerous studies have linked emotional suppression to adverse effects on mental health. Individuals who habitually suppress emotions experience higher psychological distress levels. The American Psychological Association says hidden emotions can cause physical problems like headaches and digestive issues. These issues might also lead to cardiovascular problems.

Fear of Judgment

But why do men continue to suppress their emotions despite the toll it takes on their mental health? One major factor is the fear of judgment. From a young age, men are taught to be strong, resilient, and unflappable. Expressing vulnerability is often equated with weakness, leaving men feeling vulnerable to ridicule, rejection, and shame.

The fear of judgment can come from both external sources and self-imposed expectations. Men may worry about how their friends, family, or colleagues will perceive them if they show any signs of emotional vulnerability. They may fear that opening up about their struggles will make them appear less capable.

But the fear doesn't always come from external sources. Sometimes, the biggest critic is the voice inside our heads. This inner critic might tell you that your emotions are "unmanly" or "unworthy" of being shared. This self-judgment can be just as debilitating as the fear of external judgment.

Breaking the Cycle: From Concealment to Connection

While suppressing emotions might seem like a way to protect yourself, it ultimately hinders your well-being. The good news is that you can break free from this cycle. Here are some tips:

1. Acknowledge Your Emotions: The first step is to become aware of your emotions. Pay attention to what you're feeling throughout the day, both positive and negative.

2. Challenge Negative Self-Talk: When your inner critic starts whispering doubts, challenge those thoughts. Remind yourself it's okay to feel different emotions. Expressing them shows strength, not weakness.

3. Start Small: Don't feel pressured to open up about everything at once. Start by sharing a small vulnerability with a trusted fellow

Seeking support from trusted friends, family members, or a therapist can also help alleviate the fear of judgment. Vulnerability is a shared human experience. Sharing struggles can bring empathy and connection.

Internal Conflict and Isolation

Internal Struggles

Many men silently battle between societal expectations and authentic emotional expression. The battle can lead to isolation. You may feel disconnected from yourself and others.

Society often sends a mixed message. On the one hand, men are expected to be strong, stoic figures, providers, and protectors. On the other hand, there's a growing awareness of the importance of mental health, encouraging everyone to express their emotions. This creates a confusing double bind for men – wanting to be seen as strong while also desiring emotional connection and vulnerability.

Isolation and Loneliness

Men who struggle with emotional vulnerability often feel isolated and lonely. This intensifies their internal conflict. Suppressing emotions and isolating ourselves creates barriers to connecting authentically with others. We may put up walls, keeping people at arm's length, to avoid the risk of being seen as weak or vulnerable.

Our efforts to protect ourselves end up isolating us more. We miss the chance for real connection by not sharing vulnerabilities. Sharing vulnerabilities creates intimacy and support. Instead of finding solace in solitude, we find ourselves trapped in a cycle of loneliness, longing for connection but unsure of how to break free from our self-imposed isolation.

Research underscores the detrimental effects of loneliness on mental and physical health. Loneliness is linked to various health issues. These include depression, anxiety, and cardiovascular disease. Loneliness also increases the risk of premature death. Loneliness takes a toll. It's crucial to address emotional struggles and build meaningful connections.

So how do we break free from the cycle of isolation and loneliness? It starts with vulnerability. Courageously share your struggles with trusted individuals. This helps break down barriers that isolate us. Vulnerability helps build authentic connections based on empathy, understanding, and mutual support.

Taboo Surrounding Vulnerability

We discussed men's internal conflict and societal pressure. Yet the struggle with vulnerability goes beyond individual experiences. There are deeper cultural norms and unspoken rules that create a significant barrier to men expressing their emotions openly.

Imagine you're visiting a new country with a completely different culture. Their customs, greetings, and social interactions may confuse you. There are unspoken rules, a cultural code that dictates behaviour. Unfortunately, men often face taboos about expressing emotions. This taboo involves vulnerability.

Cultural Barriers

Many cultures deeply embed male vulnerability in societal norms. From a young age, parents and society often instill in male children the expectation to be tough, stoic, and emotionally resilient. Any display of vulnerability is viewed as a sign of weakness, eliciting ridicule or dismissal. This cultural conditioning creates a barrier to open conversations about emotions, leaving many men feeling isolated and unable to express their true feelings.

Research shows that cultural norms strongly influence attitudes toward male vulnerability. Studies show that in cultures emphasizing traditional gender roles, men are less likely to seek help for emotional issues. They are also more likely to conform to traditional masculine norms. Rigid gender roles impact men's mental health and relationships. This adherence also affects their overall well-being.

Impact on Relationships

Struggling with vulnerability can deeply impact relationships, both romantic and platonic. In romantic relationships, not expressing emotions openly can cause communication breakdowns and a lack of intimacy. Partners may feel disconnected and struggle to understand each other's emotional needs. They may find it challenging to provide support.

Moreover, the taboo surrounding vulnerability can create power imbalances within relationships. One partner unable to express emotions may burden the other with providing support without reciprocation. This imbalance can strain the relationship and lead to resentment or dissatisfaction.

In platonic relationships, the impact of the hidden struggle with vulnerability is equally significant. Friendships may suffer when men feel unable to share their true feelings with their friends. This lack of emotional connection can lead to shallow or superficial relationships, leaving men feeling isolated and misunderstood.

Practical Advice

To overcome cultural barriers and taboos on vulnerability, you need courage and self-awareness. Here are some practical steps you can take to navigate these challenges:

1. Challenge Gender Stereotypes: Question traditional notions of masculinity and challenge societal expectations that dictate men should be emotionally stoic. Embrace the idea that vulnerability is a strength, not a weakness.

2. Create a safe environment. Encourage open conversations about emotions. Practice active listening and validate each other's feelings without judgment.

3. Seek support: Be bold and reach out for help when needed. Whether it's talking to a trusted friend, seeking therapy, or joining a support group, seeking support can help you navigate the challenges of vulnerability.

4. Cultivate Empathy: Practice empathy towards yourself and others. Understand that vulnerability is a universal human experience and that showing compassion towards yourself and others can help break down barriers and foster deeper connections.

By challenging cultural barriers and embracing vulnerability, you can create more authentic and fulfilling relationships, both romantically and platonically.

Action Plan for Empowering Emotional Vulnerability

Reflective Exercises

To begin your journey towards embracing emotional vulnerability, take some time to reflect on your personal experiences with emotional suppression. Find a quiet space where you can be alone with your thoughts, and consider the following questions:

1. What societal expectations or cultural norms have influenced my views on masculinity and emotional expression?

2. How have I experienced the pressure to conform to traditional ideas of masculinity, and how has this impacted my ability to authenticate my emotions?

3. Can I identify any specific instances where I have suppressed or hidden my true feelings? What were the circumstances surrounding these experiences?

4. What emotions do I find most difficult to express, and why do I think this is the case?

5. How do I believe embracing emotional vulnerability could positively impact my relationships, my work life, and my overall well-being?

Take your time with these reflections and allow yourself to be honest and introspective. By gaining a deeper understanding of your own experiences with emotional suppression, you can begin to unravel the hidden struggles that may be holding you back.

Journaling

Journaling can be a powerful tool for exploring your emotions in a private and introspective setting. Use the following prompts to guide your journaling practice:

1. Describe a recent situation where you felt pressure to hide or suppress your emotions. How did you respond in that moment, and how did it make you feel?

2. Reflect on a time when you allowed yourself to be vulnerable with someone else. What was the outcome of that experience, and how did it impact your relationship?

3. Write about a particular emotion that you find challenging to express. What are the underlying reasons behind your difficulty expressing this emotion?

4. Imagine a world where vulnerability is celebrated as strength. How would your life be different in this ideal scenario, and what steps can you take to move closer to this reality?

5. Consider the role of community support in embracing emotional vulnerability. How can you seek out supportive communities, both online and in-person, to share your experiences and find solidarity with others on a similar journey?

Commit to a regular journaling practice, whether it's daily, weekly, or whenever you feel the need to explore your emotions more deeply. Allow yourself the freedom to express your thoughts and feelings without judgment, knowing that your journal is a safe space for self-reflection and growth.

Building a Support System:

Surrounding yourself with supportive people who value vulnerability is crucial. Here's how to find your tribe:

1. Seek Out Like-Minded Individuals: Look for online communities or support groups specifically focused on men's

emotional well-being. Connecting with others who understand your struggles can be incredibly empowering.

2. Talk to a Therapist: A therapist can provide a safe space to explore your emotions and develop healthy coping mechanisms for emotional expression.

3. Open Up to Close Friends: Identify a trusted friend or family member whom you feel comfortable opening up to emotionally. Sharing your vulnerabilities can strengthen your bond and foster deeper connections.

Remember that you are not alone in your journey towards embracing emotional vulnerability. By actively engaging with supportive communities and seeking professional guidance when needed, you can cultivate greater self-awareness, resilience, and authenticity in your life

Key Takeaways

- Acknowledging the hidden struggle with emotional expression is the first step towards embracing vulnerability.

- Societal expectations and internal conflicts can significantly impact how men express their emotions

- Vulnerability is power: It takes courage to open up, but it strengthens relationships and fosters deeper connections

- Societal expectations and internal conflicts can significantly impact how men express their emotions.

- Recognizing the psychological impact of emotional suppression is crucial for overall well-being.

- Build your support system, and find communities or individuals who value vulnerability and authenticity.

- Reflection matters. Explore your experiences and identify what influences your emotional expression.

Now that you understand the hidden struggles and conflicts that are a result of the societal expectations of the vulnerable man, it's time to take deliberate action.

Reflect on past experiences, find supportive connections, and challenge the fear of vulnerability. Dive deeper into the next chapter. and discover how embracing your emotions can transform your life.

Chapter 2: The Power of Vulnerability

Vulnerability means being open to attack or harm. It can be physical or emotional. It's the willingness to expose our innermost feelings, fears, and insecurities. Allowing vulnerability creates space for genuine connections, empathy, and growth. Acknowledging vulnerability isn't a weakness. It's a courageous step towards understanding ourselves and others. Vulnerabilities invite compassion. It fosters resilience. Share your struggles with a friend. Admit limitations. Remember, it's okay to be vulnerable—it's where our strength lies.

Vulnerability fosters authentic connections, deep empathy, and personal growth. Individuals demonstrate courage by sharing their true selves. Genuine relationships are built on trust and understanding through embracing vulnerability. Vulnerability opens the door to healing, as it encourages honesty and emotional expression. It dismantles barriers to intimacy, fostering a sense of belonging and acceptance. Through vulnerability, individuals cultivate resilience and self-awareness, discovering strength in their authenticity. Moments of vulnerability lead to profound transformation. This results in greater empathy, connection, and a more meaningful life.

This chapter explores vulnerability's transformative power. Vulnerability is a courageous act. It fosters authentic connections and emotional intelligence. You will learn how to express emotions effectively. You will also learn how to create space for vulnerability in relationships. You will understand the positive impact of vulnerability. This will inspire you to embrace your authentic self. There is also an action plan to incorporate vulnerability into your life. This plan will empower you and showcase vulnerability's transformative power.

Redefining Vulnerability

Have you ever held back from expressing a genuine emotion because you worried it would be perceived as a weakness? It could have been sadness after a breakup, anxiety before a presentation, or fear during a conversation. Society often forces us to believe that showing emotions makes us seem weak. Emotions beyond happiness or confidence are particularly discouraged. But vulnerability wasn't a weakness but a hidden strength.

Strength in Vulnerability

The truth is that embracing vulnerability takes courage. It requires the strength to shed the masks we wear and expose our authentic selves, flaws and all. Consider the experience of public speaking. Stepping onto a stage and sharing your ideas in front of a crowd requires a certain level of confidence. Have you seen a speaker pause in their presentation to share a personal story or moment of vulnerability? Perhaps they confessed to feeling nervous or acknowledged a past struggle related to the topic. These moments of vulnerability can be incredibly powerful. They connect the speaker to the audience on a deeper level, fostering a sense of authenticity and genuineness that resonates far more than a perfectly scripted presentation.

Researchers at the University of Houston found that leaders who show vulnerability are more trustworthy and effective with their teams. The study suggests that vulnerability fosters a sense of connection and psychological safety within a group, ultimately leading to better collaboration and performance. So, the next time you feel a surge of vulnerability rising, don't push it down. Acknowledge it as a sign of your strength and courage to be authentic, even when it feels uncomfortable.

Research by Brené Brown, a leading expert on vulnerability, highlights the connection between vulnerability and courage. Her studies show that people viewed as more confident and authentic embrace their full range of emotions. They tend to have stronger relationships and are better at navigating life's challenges.

Let's face it, life isn't always sunshine and rainbows. We all experience sadness, anger, fear, and disappointment. Suppressing these emotions isn't healthy.

Courageous Transparency

Vulnerability isn't just about expressing negative emotions; it's about being genuine in all aspects of your life. Consider a situation where you're forced to work with someone you don't particularly like. The easy route might be to put on a fake smile and pretend everything is fine. But what if you were vulnerable, expressing your discomfort respectfully?

This act of transparency could open the door to a more honest and productive working relationship. It shows that you're a real person with genuine feelings, not just a robot programmed to get the job done. This authenticity fosters trust and respect, creating a more positive work environment for everyone.

Vulnerability is courageous transparency. It means showing up authentically, flaws and all. When we embrace vulnerability, we invite others to do the same. Authentic relationships are built on honesty and openness, and vulnerability is the key that unlocks the door to genuine connections. It's through vulnerability that we cultivate trust and understanding, fostering deeper, more meaningful relationships.

Practical Strategies for Vulnerability

We've established that vulnerability is a strength, not a weakness. But how do you translate that knowledge into action? How do you move from hiding your emotions to expressing them healthily and authentically? This section will explore practical strategies to bridge the gap between theory and practice, fostering emotional intelligence, open communication, and a mindful approach to vulnerability.

1. Emotional Intelligence: Recognizing and Expressing Your Feelings

The first step towards vulnerability is understanding your own emotions. This might sound cliche, but many of us go through life on autopilot, disconnected from our internal world.

Emotional intelligence (EQ) is the ability to recognize, understand, and manage your own emotions, as well as those of others.

Think about a time you felt overwhelmed or angry. Were you able to identify the source of your emotions? Did you healthily express them? Developing your EQ can help you answer these questions.

Here are some practical strategies to enhance your emotional intelligence:

- Mindfulness Meditation: Mindfulness practices, like meditation, help you become more aware of your thoughts and emotions without judgment. Taking a few minutes each day to simply focus on your breath and observe your emotions can be a powerful tool for self-awareness.

- Journaling: Journaling is another excellent way to explore your emotions. Writing down your thoughts and feelings can help you identify patterns and triggers, and gain a deeper understanding of your inner world.

- Identifying Body Cues: Our bodies often communicate our emotions before our minds catch up. Learn to recognize physical signs of anxiety, anger, or sadness - a racing heart, clenched fists, or a tightness in your chest. This awareness can help you identify your emotions at the moment and choose healthy ways to express them.

2. Open Communication Skills: Creating Space for Vulnerability

Once you understand your emotions, it's time to express them effectively. Here's where open communication skills come into play. Open communication involves honest and respectful dialogue, where both partners feel safe expressing their feelings.

Here are some key communication techniques to foster vulnerability:

- Active Listening: Pay close attention to what the other person is saying, both verbally and nonverbally. Avoid interrupting and make eye contact to show you're engaged.

- "I" Statements: Instead of blaming or accusing language, use "I" statements to express your emotions. For example, instead of saying, "You always make me feel bad," try, "I feel hurt when you..." This approach focuses on your feelings and reduces defensiveness toward the other person.

- Validate Their Feelings: Acknowledge the other person's emotions and let them know their feelings are valid. This creates a safe space for them to express themselves openly.

Psychological Benefits of Vulnerability

Remember the last time you confided in a friend about a deep worry or a personal setback? Did sharing that burden lift a weight off your shoulders? Or perhaps, have you ever witnessed someone open up about their struggles and, in turn, felt a surge of connection and understanding? These are just a few of the remarkable benefits of vulnerability – reduced stress and increased empathy.

Vulnerability as a Stress-Buster

Research published in the journal Psychosomatic Medicine reveals a fascinating connection between vulnerability and stress reduction. The study found that individuals who practiced vulnerability by expressing their emotions openly experienced lower levels of stress hormones like cortisol.

Here's why vulnerability helps you manage stress:

- Release and Regulation: Bottling up emotions is like stuffing a balloon; eventually, the pressure builds, and it pops. Vulnerability allows you to release those pent-up emotions healthily. By expressing your feelings, you can begin to process and regulate them, leading to a calmer and more centered state of mind.

- Social Support System: When you open up to a trusted friend or family member, you create an opportunity for support. Sharing your struggles allows them to offer empathy, understanding, and practical help. This social support system can be a powerful buffer against stress.

- Self-Compassion: Vulnerability can also foster self-compassion. By acknowledging your emotions and accepting yourself as a human being with flaws and vulnerabilities, you can develop a kinder and more understanding relationship with yourself. This self-compassion reduces stress and promotes emotional well-being.

The Empathy Advantage

Vulnerability isn't just good for you; it's good for your relationships, and one of the most beautiful aspects of vulnerability is its ability to foster empathy. Empathy is the ability to understand and share the feelings of others. When you open up about your struggles, you create a space for others to do the same. This shared vulnerability strengthens connections and builds a sense of "we're all in this together."

A study published in the Journal of Personality and Social Psychology explored the link between vulnerability and empathy. The study found that individuals who disclosed personal information about themselves were perceived as more empathetic and trustworthy by others.

Here's how vulnerability strengthens relationships through empathy:

- Deeper Connections: Vulnerability allows you to connect with others on a deeper level. By sharing your authentic self, you create a sense of intimacy and trust that fosters stronger bonds.

- Improved Communication: Open communication is crucial for healthy relationships. When you're vulnerable with someone, you're more likely to communicate your needs and feelings effectively. This leads to less conflict and a deeper sense of understanding between partners.

- Building Trust: Vulnerability requires trust. When you open up to someone, you're essentially placing your trust in them. This act of trust strengthens the bond and creates a safe space for both partners to be vulnerable.

Vulnerability in the Workplace

The benefits of vulnerability extend beyond personal relationships. Research suggests that vulnerability can also have a positive impact on professional relationships. A study published in the Harvard Business Review found that leaders who displayed vulnerability by admitting mistakes and expressing emotions were perceived as more authentic and relatable by their employees. This, in turn, led to increased employee engagement and productivity.

The Ripple Effect of Vulnerability

The benefits of vulnerability extend far beyond the individual. When you embrace vulnerability and build strong, empathetic relationships, you create a ripple effect. These positive connections foster a more supportive and compassionate environment, impacting everyone around you.

Imagine a workplace where employees feel comfortable expressing their concerns and challenges. This vulnerability can lead to a more collaborative and productive environment. Or consider a community where individuals openly share their struggles. This openness can foster a sense of belonging and support, leading to a stronger and more resilient community.

By embracing vulnerability, you not only reduce your stress and increase your empathy, but you also contribute to a more positive and connected world.

Action Plan for Embracing Emotional Vulnerabilities

The world often praises strength and resilience but shames vulnerability. It's hard to be open and authentic.

This section provides an action plan to guide you in embracing vulnerability. Reflect on past experiences. Practice transparent communication. Engage in a mindful vulnerability challenge. Journal for reflection. Unlock vulnerability's potential. Build a fulfilling life.

Reflecting on Vulnerability's Strength

Let's take a moment for some introspection. Think back to a time in your life when you were vulnerable. Perhaps you opened up to a friend about a personal struggle, shared a hidden fear with a loved one, or expressed gratitude to someone who made a difference in your life.

- How did your vulnerability impact the outcome of the situation?

- Did it lead to a deeper connection with the other person?

- Did you experience a sense of relief or catharsis from expressing your true emotions?

Jot down your reflections in a journal or discuss them with a trusted friend. By reflecting on past experiences of vulnerability, you can reframe it as a strength, something that enhances your relationships and enriches your life. This awareness can empower you to embrace vulnerability with greater confidence in the future.

The Power of Transparent Communication

Effective communication is the cornerstone of healthy relationships. Vulnerability plays a crucial role in achieving transparent communication. But how do you translate your emotions into clear and honest communication?

Transparent communication takes practice. Start by incorporating these techniques into small conversations with friends and family. The more you practice, the easier it becomes to express your emotions openly and honestly.

Mindful Vulnerability Challenge

Are you ready to take your vulnerability to the next level? Here's a week-long challenge to help you integrate vulnerability into different aspects of your life:

- **Day 1:** Compliment a Stranger: Step outside your comfort zone and compliment someone you don't know well. This simple act of vulnerability can brighten their day and spark a positive interaction.

- **Day 2:** Share a Concern with a Loved One: Do you have a concern regarding a relationship with a friend or family member? Schedule some time to have a heart-to-heart conversation. Express your feelings honestly and listen openly to their perspective.

- **Day 3:** Write a Heartfelt Letter: Take some time to write a letter expressing gratitude or appreciation to someone who has made a significant impact on your life. The act of expressing your emotions in writing can be a powerful form of vulnerability.

- **Day 4:** Practice Active Listening with Empathy: During a conversation with a friend or colleague, actively listen to their emotions. Show empathy by validating their feelings and offering support if needed.

- **Day 5:** Express a Fear: Have you been holding onto a secret fear? Share this fear with a trusted friend or therapist. Expressing your vulnerabilities can be liberating and help you gain a new perspective.

- **Day 6:** Ask for Help: We all need help sometimes. Don't be afraid to ask for assistance when you need it. Doing so demonstrates vulnerability and allows others to offer support.

- **Day 7:** Journal your Reflections: Take some time to reflect on your week-long vulnerability challenge. Did you notice any changes in your relationships or emotional well-being? Journaling these reflections will help you understand the impact of vulnerability in your life.

This challenge is designed to empower you to step outside your comfort zone and engage in intentional vulnerability. Remember, vulnerability is not a one-time event; it's an ongoing process. The more you practice, the more comfortable you'll become with expressing your true emotions.

Journaling for Deeper Insights

Journaling is a powerful tool for self-discovery and reflection. Throughout this week, take some time after each vulnerability challenge to document your experiences in your journal. Here are some prompts to guide your reflections:

- How did expressing vulnerability make you feel (anxious, relieved, or empowered)?

- Did you notice any changes in your relationships with others?

- Did you experience any unexpected outcomes from your vulnerability?

- What did you learn about yourself from this experience?

By journaling your reflections, you can gain valuable insights into the impact of vulnerability on your emotional well-being, relationships, and overall sense of self.

Key Takeaways

- Strength in Vulnerability: Embracing your full range of emotions is a courageous act, not a weakness.

- Transparency Builds Bridges: Vulnerability fosters deeper connections by creating a space for courageous transparency.

- Emotional Intelligence Matters: Understanding your emotions is the first step towards expressing them effectively.

- Open Communication is Key: Effective communication is the cornerstone of healthy relationships, and vulnerability plays a crucial role in achieving transparent communication

- Mindfulness for Clarity: Mindfulness practices can help you manage strong emotions and express them clearly.

- Vulnerability Reduces Stress: Bottling up emotions can lead to stress; expressing them can be liberating.

- Deeper Connections: Vulnerability allows you to connect with others on a deeper, more meaningful level.

- Personal Growth: Expressing your true self opens doors for personal growth and a more fulfilling life.

Are you ready to embrace your vulnerability? This week, put the learnings into action with our mindful vulnerability challenge. In the next chapter, we'll explore redefining male empathy in a cultural context, and we'll also unlock strategies for a more emotionally authentic future.

Chapter 3: Emotional Vulnerability in Relationships

Imagine a world where expressing your true feelings isn't seen as a weakness but as a sign of strength. A world where men feel comfortable sharing their hopes, fears, and vulnerabilities with their partners, fostering deeper connections and a more fulfilling love life. This world is within reach, but it requires a shift in perspective—a redefinition of male empathy in our cultural context. Men should feel comfortable sharing their hopes, fears, and vulnerabilities.

Throughout history, societal expectations have often discouraged men from expressing their emotions openly.

This chapter explores how expectations affect male empathy in close relationships. We'll explore how embracing vulnerability can strengthen the emotional connection, communication, and trust between partners. We'll also address the challenges men face in navigating vulnerability and provide practical strategies to foster a more emotionally authentic and fulfilling romantic life.

Understanding the Impact of Emotional Vulnerability

Enhanced Emotional Intimacy

Intimacy goes beyond physical closeness. It's about feeling truly seen, heard, and understood by your partner. Vulnerability—the act of expressing your true emotions, both positive and negative, creates a space for this deeper connection to flourish.

In a published journal about personality and social relationships. Researchers discovered that couples who shared feelings and experiences reported higher levels of intimacy. They also reported greater relationship satisfaction.

Here's how vulnerability fosters emotional intimacy:

1. Creating a Safe Space: When you open up about your vulnerabilities, you invite your partner to do the same. This reciprocal exchange brings about a sense of safety and trust. You're saying, "I trust you enough to show you my true self, imperfections and all." This creates a safe haven for open communication and emotional connection.

2. Strengthening Emotional Bonds: Sharing your vulnerabilities allows your partner to connect with you on a deeper level. Imagine confiding in your partner about a childhood trauma. Their empathy and understanding create a

stronger emotional bond. They see beyond the surface, connecting with your inner world. This then creates a sense of closeness and intimacy that transcends the superficial.

3. Validation and Acceptance: Vulnerability allows your partner to validate your emotions. A supportive partner acknowledges your feelings, letting you know you're not alone. Validation fosters a sense of acceptance and belonging, deepening the emotional connection between you.

Transforming Communication Dynamics

Communication is the lifeblood of any relationship. But sometimes, unspoken emotions and unspoken needs can create misunderstandings and distance. Vulnerability can be the key to unlocking more effective communication.

1. Honest Expression: Vulnerability allows you to express your feelings honestly without bottling them up or resorting to passive-aggressiveness. This creates a space for open and direct communication, reducing the chances of misunderstandings.

2. Conflict Resolution: When disagreements arise, vulnerability can help navigate them more constructively. Sharing how a situation makes you feel allows your partner to understand your perspective and respond with empathy.

3. Strengthened Problem-Solving: By openly communicating your needs and concerns, you and your partner can work together to find solutions to problems. This collaborative

approach fosters a sense of teamwork and strengthens your relationship.

Building a Foundation of Trust

Trust is the cornerstone of any healthy relationship. Vulnerability plays a critical role in building and strengthening this foundation.

1. Emotional Availability: When you open yourself up emotionally, you demonstrate trust in your partner. This creates a sense of security and allows the relationship to flourish. When you share a deeply personal secret with your partner, their supportive response and willingness to hold this information safely reinforce trust.

2. Creating a Sense of Security: Vulnerability fosters a sense of security in a relationship. By sharing your vulnerabilities, you make yourself open to your partner's support. This creates a sense of mutual reliance and strengthens the feeling of being in a safe and supportive space.

3. Greater Vulnerability, Greater Trust: The cycle of vulnerability and trust is reciprocal. The more you share your true self, the more trust you build. This increased trust, in turn, allows you to be even more vulnerable, creating a positive feedback loop that deepens your connection with your partner.

Challenges in Navigating Intimate Connections

We've explored how vulnerability can spice up deeper connections in romantic relationships. But let's be honest, embracing vulnerability isn't always sunshine and rainbows. There are challenges to navigate, and it's important to acknowledge these hurdles before taking the plunge.

Fear of Rejection

The fear of rejection is perhaps the biggest obstacle to vulnerability. Sharing your true feelings leaves you exposed, and the possibility of your partner not reciprocating can be daunting. This fear stems from a fundamental human need for connection and belonging. Rejection, in this context, feels like a threat to those core needs.

Here's how to overcome the fear of rejection and embrace vulnerability:

- Reframing Rejection: Rejection doesn't have to be a permanent roadblock. Sometimes, it's simply a sign of incompatibility. View rejection as an opportunity for growth and a chance to find a partner who truly appreciates your vulnerability.

- Start Small: You don't have to pour your heart out on the first date. Start by sharing small vulnerabilities, gradually building your comfort level. This allows your partner to reciprocate your openness, fostering a sense of emotional safety.

- Focus on the Potential Gains: Instead of dwelling on the potential for rejection, focus on the potential rewards of vulnerability. A deeper connection, stronger trust, and a more fulfilling relationship are all within reach.

- Celebrate Vulnerability Victories: Acknowledge and celebrate your progress. Each time you express a vulnerability, no matter how small, it's a victory over your fear.

Vulnerability Imbalance

Imagine you're excitedly sharing your hopes and dreams with your partner, but their response is muted or dismissive. This imbalance in vulnerability can create tension and strain in a relationship.

Here's why:

- Feeling Unheard and Unsupported: The partner who is more open emotionally may feel unheard or unsupported if their vulnerability isn't reciprocated. This can lead to feelings of frustration and resentment.

- Pressure to Conform: The less vulnerable partner may feel pressured to conform to their partner's level of emotional expression. This can lead to inauthenticity and a sense of suffocation in the relationship.

211

- The Blame Game: When vulnerability isn't balanced, blame can easily creep in. The more vulnerable partner may blame the other for not being open enough, creating a vicious cycle of negativity.

Strategies for Achieving Balanced Vulnerability

1. Open Communication is Key: Talk to your partner about your desired level of vulnerability in the relationship. Communicate your needs and listen openly to theirs.

2. Respect Individual Differences: People have different comfort levels with vulnerability. Respect your partner's pace and encourage them to gradually step outside their comfort zone.

3. Focus on Mutual Growth: Frame vulnerability as a journey you're taking together. Celebrate each other's progress and create a safe space for both partners to explore their emotional landscapes.

4. Lead by Example: If you want your partner to be more vulnerable, be a role model.

Express your own vulnerabilities authentically and show them the emotional rewards of openness.

By addressing these challenges and building an environment of mutual respect and understanding, you can navigate the vulnerability tightrope and create a more fulfilling and connected relationship.

Real-Life Couples: Vulnerability as a Bridge to Deeper Connection

One Sunday evening, I decided to organize a brunch with my close friends, all married couples. The brunch's main purpose was for each couple to share their relationship journeys. They discussed the challenges they faced and how they navigated them.

We discussed emotional vulnerability's impact on relationships. Men's struggle to open up was a key focus.

Here are some of their stories:

1. Jessica & Ethan: From Frustration to Forgiveness

Jessica, a successful lawyer, found herself constantly frustrated by Ethan's emotionless demeanor. After months of bottling up her feelings, she decided to have an honest conversation. Tears streamed down her face as she confessed feeling unheard and emotionally distant. Ethan, initially taken aback, listened intently without interrupting. He then surprised her by sharing his struggles—a fear of failure he'd never spoken of before. This shared vulnerability opened a floodgate of emotions. They spent hours talking, offering comfort and understanding. The next morning, they woke up feeling closer than ever before. The experience strengthened their bond. It taught them the importance of creating a safe space for emotional expression.

2. David & Alex: Career Dreams and Relationship Realities

David, an aspiring writer, felt increasingly burdened by the financial pressure of supporting their family. He harbored a secret dream of pursuing his writing full-time, but fear of Alex's disapproval kept him silent. One evening, after a particularly stressful day, he decided to take a chance. He confessed his anxieties and his long-held dream. Alex, instead of being dismissive, surprised him with her unwavering support. She acknowledged his sacrifices and expressed her belief in his talent. This shared vulnerability allowed them to have a difficult but honest conversation about their finances and priorities. Together, they came up with a plan to support David's writing dream while ensuring their family's stability.

3. Sarah & Michael: Overcoming Past Hurts

Sarah, recently out of a long-term relationship, found it difficult to trust Michael fully. Memories of past betrayals left her guarded and hesitant to open up emotionally. One night, after a fight, Michael took a different approach. Instead of getting defensive, he shared his vulnerabilities about past relationship insecurities. This unexpected move disarmed Sarah. She began to share her fears, and they spent the night talking openly and honestly. This shared vulnerability created a space for healing and forgiveness. Sarah started to trust Michael more deeply, and their relationship blossomed.

These real-life stories illustrate the transformative power of shared vulnerability. When both partners are willing to open up emotionally, it creates a ripple effect:

- Deeper Understanding: Sharing your vulnerabilities allows your partner to see the world from your perspective. This fosters empathy and a deeper understanding of your emotional landscape.

- Strengthened Trust: Reciprocal vulnerability is a cornerstone of trust. By opening yourself up emotionally, you demonstrate your trust in your partner's ability to handle your true feelings. This trust, in turn, strengthens the foundation of your relationship.

- Greater Intimacy: Shared vulnerability allows you to connect with your partner on a deeper and more meaningful level. You create a safe space for emotional intimacy where both partners feel seen, heard, and understood.

A healthy relationship thrives on reciprocity. While one partner initiating vulnerability is a positive step, it's crucial to encourage a two-way flow of emotions.

Here's why reciprocity matters:

- Balanced Connection: A relationship where only one partner expresses vulnerabilities becomes lopsided and unsustainable. Reciprocity creates a balanced dynamic where both partners feel comfortable sharing their emotions.

- Mutual Respect and Support: When both partners are vulnerable, it demonstrates a sense of mutual respect and support. You're essentially saying, "I trust you enough to share my vulnerabilities, and I'm here for yours too."

- Emotional Growth Together: The journey of vulnerability is a shared experience. By encouraging each other to step outside your comfort zones, you can both grow emotionally and create a more fulfilling relationship.

Remember, reciprocity doesn't mean forcing your partner to share at your pace. It's about creating a safe and supportive environment where they feel comfortable expressing their vulnerabilities in their own time.

By embracing shared vulnerability, you can build a bridge of trust, understanding, and intimacy, creating a more fulfilling and connected relationship.

Level Up with This Vulnerability Game: Creative Exercises for Couples

We've covered the foundational aspects of vulnerability in relationships. Now, let's dive into some engaging exercises that go beyond the typical conversation starters. These activities are designed to spark deeper connections and encourage vulnerability in a fun and creative way:

1. **The "36 Questions" Exercise:** Developed by psychologist Arthur Aron, this set of 36 increasingly personal questions is designed to foster intimacy and connection. Take turns asking each other the questions, offering honest and open answers.
   Download here:
   https://amorebeautifulquestion.com/wp-content/uploads/2024/02/Arthur-Arons-36-questions-2.pdf

2. The "Dear Younger You" Letter: This exercise takes inspiration from childhood memories. Grab a pen and paper and write a letter to your younger self, addressing any insecurities or challenges you faced. Then, share this letter with your partner. This act of vulnerability allows you to explore your emotional landscape and fosters empathy from your partner.

3. The "Vulnerability Jar": Turn vulnerability into a playful challenge. Take a jar and decorate it together. Throughout the week, write down moments where you felt vulnerable, either positive or negative (e.g., "I opened up about my anxieties about work"). At the end of the week, pick a random note from the jar and discuss the experience with your partner. his injects an element of surprise and encourages open communication.

4. The "Strength Through Vulnerability" Collage: This activity is a powerful visual representation of your emotional journey. Create a collage together using magazine clippings, photos, or drawings. Include images that represent moments of vulnerability in your relationship, alongside images that symbolize the strength and growth that emerged from those experiences. Discuss the collage together, reflecting on your shared journey of vulnerability.

5. The "Non-Verbal Vulnerability Challenge": Sometimes, words can be limiting. Dedicate an evening to expressing vulnerabilities through non-verbal cues. This could involve acting out a scenario where you felt vulnerable, creating a piece of art that reflects your emotions, or writing a short poem for each other. This exercise encourages emotional expression beyond words and can lead to a deeper understanding.

6. The "Gratitude Walk": Combine gratitude with vulnerability for a powerful bonding experience. Take a walk together in nature and take turns expressing things you appreciate about each other, your relationship, or yourselves. This fosters a sense of positivity and creates a space for deeper emotional connection.

Remember, the key is to find what works best for you as a couple. Embrace creativity, have fun with these exercises, and most importantly, celebrate each other's vulnerabilities. By stepping outside your comfort zones together, you'll strengthen your bond and create a more fulfilling relationship.

Key Takeaways

- Vulnerability fosters deeper emotional intimacy by creating a safe space for genuine connection.

- Open communication thrives on vulnerability, leading to more honest and productive conversations.

- Vulnerability strengthens trust by demonstrating your faith in your partner's ability to handle your emotions.

- Fear of rejection and vulnerability imbalances can hinder emotional connection – address these challenges openly.

- Shared vulnerability, a two-way street, fosters deeper understanding, strengthens trust, and creates a more fulfilling relationship.

- Utilize exercises like the "36 Questions" to build a safe space for vulnerability.

- Spice things up with creative exercises like the "Dear Younger You Letter" or the "Vulnerability Jar" to explore vulnerability playfully.

- Non-verbal exercises like creating art or poems together can encourage deeper emotional expression.

- Gratitude walks promote positivity and create a space for deeper emotional connection in your relationship.

By implementing these strategies, you'll enhance intimacy and foster a healthier relationship. Ready to unlock the full potential of emotions? Dive into the next chapter for insights on mastering emotional expression. The chapter offers actionable advice for your relationship

Chapter 4: The Language of Emotions

Have you ever felt overwhelmed by emotions but couldn't express them clearly? Perhaps you ended up saying something you didn't mean, or the other person completely misinterpreted your feelings. This is where mastering the language of emotions becomes crucial. Just like any other language, emotions have their own vocabulary and communication styles.

Trying to have a complex conversation in a foreign language with only a few words makes it hard to convey the correct message. That's what it's like when your emotional vocabulary is limited. Develop your emotional fluency. This helps you understand your feelings and communicate effectively in relationships. You'll be able to move beyond simple labels like "happy" or "sad" and express a wider range of emotions with precision. This new fluency will help you build better connections. It will also help you handle disagreements well. You can create a more satisfying emotional landscape in every part of your life.

With this chapter, you will be able to understand and express your emotions effectively. You will see the importance of emotional vocabulary, explore diverse communication styles, and offer practical exercises to enhance your emotional expression. Get ready to unlock the transformative power of emotional intelligence and build stronger, more meaningful connections.

Understanding the Language of Emotions

Emotions are the vibrant hues that paint the canvas of our lives. Emotions shape experiences, influence decisions, and connect people. Yet, how often do we pause to truly understand how our feelings work?

Imagine emotions as words—each one carrying a distinct shade, texture, and resonance. A broad emotional vocabulary lets us express subtle feelings. It's like having a broader palette to paint with, allowing us to create emotional masterpieces.

Why Does Emotional Vocabulary Matter?

- Precision in Expression: When we label an emotion, we give it form and substance. Instead of merely feeling "off," we can say, "I'm feeling anxious." This specificity helps us communicate more effectively with others and ourselves.

- Self-Awareness: Emotional literacy—the ability to recognize, described, and understand feelings—enhances self-awareness. It's like turning on a light in the dimly lit corridors of our psyche. We become attuned to the subtle shifts within us.

- Emotional Regulation: Imagine having a toolbox filled with tools for different tasks. Emotional vocabulary is one such tool. When we can describe our emotions, we have control over them. We can soothe anxiety, channel anger constructively, and savor joy consciously.

Emotional Vocabulary and Well-Being: The Science Behind It

A study in the Journal of Personality and Social Psychology shows that people with a broad emotional vocabulary have higher emotional well-being.

Here's what they discovered:

1. Negative Emotion Vocabulary and Distress:

People who use a wider variety of negative emotional words tend to display signs of lower well-being.

These signs include references to illness, loneliness, and other signs of psychological distress.

Individuals with an extensive negative emotion vocabulary experience more depression and neuroticism. They also have worse physical health.

2. Positive Emotion Vocabulary and Flourishing:

People who use positive emotional words show signs of well-being.

These signs include references to leisure activities, achievements, and belonging to a group.

People with a broad positive emotion vocabulary tend to have higher conscientiousness, extraversion, and agreeableness.

They also enjoy better overall health and experience lower rates of depression and neuroticism.

Building Your Emotional Vocabulary

Ready to embark on your journey to emotional fluency? Here are some practical tips to expand your emotional vocabulary:

1. Pay attention to the subtle emotions you experience daily. Instead of labeling everything as "good" or "bad," try to identify the specific feeling. Are you feeling frustrated, anxious, or perhaps a sense of accomplishment?

2. Read Literature and Watch Films: Pay attention to how authors and filmmakers depict a range of emotions through their characters' words and actions. This can inspire you to expand your own emotional vocabulary.

Beyond Words: Exploring Expressive Communication Styles

Not everyone expresses emotions verbally. Some people are naturally more expressive through body language, facial expressions, or creative outlets. Recognizing your own communication style and that of those around you is key to effective emotional expression:

- The Verbal Expresser: These individuals readily express their emotions through words. They might initiate conversations about their feelings and readily share their thoughts and opinions.

- The Non-verbal Expresser: These people communicate emotions more through their body language, facial expressions, and tone of voice. Paying close attention to these nonverbal cues is crucial to understanding their feelings.

- The Creative Expresser: Some individuals find solace in expressing emotions through creative outlets like art, music, or writing. These activities can be powerful tools for emotional release and self-exploration.

Understanding Your Communication Style

Reflect on how you typically express your emotions. Do you find yourself talking things through, or do you withdraw and process internally? Perhaps you gravitate towards creative expression to navigate complex emotions. Understanding your natural style helps you choose communication methods that resonate with you. You can effectively convey your feelings to others.

Adapting Your Communication

While knowing your own style is important, effective communication often involves adapting to the communication styles of others. Here are some tips:

- Observe Nonverbal Cues: Pay attention to body language, facial expressions, and tone of voice to understand the emotional undercurrents of a conversation.

- Ask Clarifying Questions: If you're unsure about someone's emotions, don't hesitate to ask clarifying questions in a gentle and respectful manner.

- Embrace Different Forms of Expression: Recognize that others might express emotions differently than you do. Be open to understanding their unique communication style.

Expand your emotional vocabulary and recognize diverse communication styles. This will help you navigate human connections effectively. In the next section, we'll explore practical exercises to further enhance your emotional expression.

Communication Techniques for Authentic Expression

Effective emotional expression isn't just about conveying your own feelings; it's also about creating a space where others feel heard and understood. This two-way street of communication is crucial for building strong and healthy relationships.

This section covers two key techniques: active listening and "I" statements. They help you navigate conversations with more emotional intelligence.

Active Listening: The Art of Truly Hearing

Have you ever felt like you're talking to a brick wall during a conversation? Perhaps your partner seems distracted, or a friend interrupts you mid-sentence. These experiences highlight the importance of active listening, a skill that goes beyond simply hearing someone's words.

Active listening involves paying full attention to the speaker, both verbally and nonverbally. It's about creating a safe space where the other person feels comfortable expressing themselves openly and honestly. Research from the University of California, Los Angeles, suggests that active listening can foster empathy, trust, and positive communication outcomes.

Essential Elements of Active Listening:

- Give Your Full Attention: Put away distractions like your phone and make eye contact with the speaker. This conveys your interest and encourages them to continue sharing.

- Listen Verbally and Nonverbally: Pay attention to both the words being spoken and the underlying emotions conveyed through body language, facial expressions, and tone of voice.

- Use Verbal Cues: Acknowledge the speaker with nonverbal cues like head nods or brief interjections like "mm-hmm" to show you're engaged.

- Ask Clarifying Questions: Don't be afraid to ask questions to ensure you understand their perspective. Phrase your questions in a way that encourages elaboration, not judgment.

- Summarize and Reflect: Periodically summarize what you've heard to demonstrate your understanding and encourage further elaboration.

By actively listening, you create a safe space for emotional expression and show genuine care for the other person's feelings.

The Power of "I" Statements: Owning Your Emotions

Have you ever tried expressing your feelings, only to have the conversation escalate into a blame game? This is where "I" statements come in. "I" statements are a powerful tool for expressing your emotions in a way that takes ownership without placing blame on the other person.

Here's the difference:

- "You" Statement: "You always make me feel bad when you..." (This is accusatory and can shut down communication)

- "I" Statement: "I feel hurt when you..." (This focuses on your feelings and opens the door for a constructive conversation)

Benefits of Using "I" Statements:

- Promotes Self-Awareness: "I" statements encourage you to identify and acknowledge your own emotions before expressing them to others.

- Reduces Blame: By focusing on your feelings, you avoid accusatory language that can trigger defensiveness in the other person.

- Encourages Open Communication: "I" statements create a space for the other person to understand your perspective and respond constructively.

Formulating Effective "I" Statements:

Crafting clear and concise "I" statements takes practice. Here's a simple formula:

I feel (emotion) when (describe the situation). Because (explain the impact of the situation)

"I" Statements in Practice:

Imagine you're feeling frustrated because your partner keeps leaving their dirty dishes in the sink. Here's how an "I" statement can help:

"I feel frustrated (emotion) when I see dirty dishes left in the sink (describe the situation). Because I feel like I'm always the one cleaning up (explain the impact)."

This approach focuses on your feelings and opens the door for a collaborative solution.

"I" statements promote personal responsibility and accountability in communication while fostering mutual respect and validation. They encourage a collaborative approach to problem-solving and conflict resolution, creating a supportive environment where both parties feel heard and valued.

Navigating Difficult Conversations

Life is full of disagreements, hurt feelings, and misunderstandings. Difficult conversations are inevitable, but they don't have to be destructive. The solution is not to avoid tough conversations. Instead, navigate them with emotional intelligence. This ensures a productive result.

Conflict Resolution Strategies

Conflict can be a catalyst for growth and positive change. Approaching with anger, blame, or defensiveness escalates issues and prevents resolution.

Here are some strategies to navigate difficult conversations with emotional intelligence:

1. Choose the Right Time and Place: Don't initiate a heated conversation when emotions are running high. Choose a calm moment when both parties are available for a focused discussion.

2. Set the Tone: By expressing your feelings and concerns in a way that avoids blame. This helps the other person feel heard and less likely to become defensive.

3. Listen: Pay close attention to both verbal and nonverbal cues. Acknowledge their perspective and ask clarifying questions to ensure understanding.

4. Focus on Problem-Solving, Not Blame: Shift the focus from who's right or wrong to finding a solution that works for everyone involved.

5. Be Willing to Compromise: Finding common ground is key to resolving conflict. Be open to different perspectives and be

prepared to compromise to reach a mutually beneficial agreement.

The Power of Empathy

Empathy is the ability to understand and share the feelings of another person. During charged conversations, empathy is crucial for fostering understanding and building bridges.

University of California, Berkeley studies show empathy reduces negative emotions. Empathy also promotes cooperation in conflict resolution. Here are some tips to cultivate empathy in communication:

1. Listen Without Judgment: Set aside your own biases and truly try to understand the other person's perspective.

2. Validate Their Feelings: Acknowledge their emotions, even if you don't agree with them. Phrases like "It sounds like you're feeling..." can go a long way.

3. See Things from Their Perspective: Try to understand the situation from their point of view. What are their concerns? What might be driving their emotions?

Difficult conversations are an opportunity for growth and connection. Express your emotions effectively, employ conflict resolution strategies, and cultivate empathy. This way, you can navigate situations with more emotional intelligence, fostering stronger relationships.

Key Takeaways

- Unlocking Your Inner Voice: Mastering emotional expression empowers you to navigate your inner world with greater clarity and communicate your feelings authentically.

- Building Your Emotional Vocabulary: Expand your vocabulary beyond "happy" and "sad" to identify and express a wider range of emotions with precision.

- Express Yourself Beyond Words: Explore creative outlets like art, music, or writing to release and explore emotions in a unique way.

- Active Listening is Key: Pay close attention to both verbal and nonverbal cues to truly understand the emotions of others.

- "I" Statement: Utilize "I" statements to express your feelings without blame, fostering healthier communication.

- Navigating Conflict with Ease: Employ conflict resolution strategies and empathy to navigate difficult conversations productively.

- Understanding Leads to Connection: By actively listening and expressing yourself clearly, you can build stronger, more meaningful relationships.

- Problem-Solving, Not Blame Games: Focus on finding solutions that work for everyone involved during disagreements.

- Practice Makes Progress: The more you practice expressing your emotions effectively, the more comfortable and confident you'll become.

- Emotional Intelligence Empowers You: Developing your emotional intelligence equips you to face life's challenges with greater resilience and build a more fulfilling life.

Are you ready to take action? Choose one communication technique this week. Practice it daily. Perhaps you'll actively listen to a colleague with your full attention or use an "I" statement to express a concern to your manager. Remember, small changes can lead to big results in your emotional expression journey. The next chapter explores the unique challenges and opportunities of emotional expression at work, equipping you to navigate these situations with greater confidence and emotional intelligence.

Part 2: The Boardroom Balance - Applying Emotional Intelligence at Work

Chapter 5: The Workplace Dilemma

Is there always pressure to bottle up your emotions at work? You disagree with your colleague's approach during a tense negotiation. Expressing frustration could seem unprofessional at work. It might disrupt workplace harmony. Many men in professional settings often struggle with balancing authentic expression and fear of judgment. Navigating the unspoken rules at work is challenging. It underscores emotional expression challenges. This dilemma can cause stress, burnout, and strained relationships. It affects individual well-being and organizational dynamics. We will uncover strategies to navigate this challenge. We'll cultivate a work environment that values emotional authenticity.

This chapter delves into the complexities of emotional intelligence in the work sphere. We will discuss traditional work emotions, changes in emotional intelligence, and men's challenges. There are practical strategies and inspiring insights that empower you to navigate the workplace for career success.

The Emotional Landscape of the Workplace

For decades, professional settings have often prioritized logic and control. The unspoken rule? Keep your emotions in check. Passionate disagreement? Disruptive. This stoic ideal, however, comes at a cost. Let's see the traditional expectations surrounding emotional expression and explore the exciting shift towards emotional intelligence in modern workplaces.

Traditional Workplace Expectations

These expectations come from viewing the workplace as rational and objective. People viewed emotions as disruptive forces that clouded judgment and hindered productivity. This perspective created a culture favoring logic over emotions. Emotional expression was marginalized.

The consequences of this approach can be far-reaching. Stifling emotional expression can lead to:

- Miscommunication: Unexpressed emotions can fester, leading to misunderstandings and resentment between colleagues. Misinterpreted nonverbal cues can complicate communication.

- Hindered Collaboration: Innovation thrives in an environment where diverse perspectives are openly shared. When people fear judgment for expressing their true feelings, collaboration suffers, and the team misses out on valuable insights.

- Employee Disengagement: Feeling like you can't be your authentic self at work can be draining and lead to disengagement. Employees who suppress emotions may feel more stressed and less satisfied at work.

Modern workplaces increasingly recognize the value of emotional intelligence (EQ). EQ is the ability to understand, use, and manage emotions effectively. It helps individuals achieve their goals. In the workplace context, this translates to leaders and employees who can:

- Self-Awareness: Recognize their own emotions and how they impact their behavior.

- Emotional Regulation: Manage their emotions effectively, preventing them from clouding judgment.

- Motivation: Use their emotions to fuel motivation and drive results.

- Empathy: Understand and share the feelings of others, fostering stronger relationships.

- Social Skills: Build rapport, communicate effectively, and navigate conflict constructively.

The benefits of emotional intelligence in the workplace are undeniable. The Harvard Business Review studies show EQ is crucial for leadership success. EQ accounts for almost 90% of the top performers. Organizations with emotionally intelligent employees experience:

- Team members' open expression boosts collaboration and efficiency in problem-solving.

- Enhanced Innovation: A diverse range of perspectives, freely expressed, leads to more creative solutions and a competitive edge.

- Improved Conflict Resolution: EQ allows individuals to address disagreements constructively, focusing on solutions rather than blame.

- Positive Work Environment: Open communication and mutual respect foster a sense of trust and belonging, leading to higher employee engagement and satisfaction.

The traditional workplace may have valued stoicism, but the modern landscape demands a shift. Emotional intelligence is no longer a "soft skill" but a crucial asset for success. By building an environment where emotional expression is encouraged and emotional intelligence is valued, organizations can unlock the full potential of their workforce and create a thriving workplace culture.

Challenges Men Encounter in Emotional Expression at Work

For many men, expressing emotions beyond happiness or anger can carry a social stigma. Tears might be seen as weakness, frustration as unprofessional, and even excitement as childish. These stereotypes can be incredibly limiting, preventing men from expressing their full range of emotions and hindering genuine connection with colleagues.

The science behind emotions is clear: they are not signs of weakness but natural human responses. Studies by the American Psychological Association (APA) show that suppressing emotions can have negative consequences for our health.

This perception can lead to a self-silencing effect, hindering men from openly communicating their feelings and hindering their ability to connect with colleagues on a deeper level.

The consequences of these stereotypes can be significant:

1. Fear of Judgment: The fear of being perceived as weak or unprofessional can prevent men from voicing concerns, seeking help, or celebrating successes with genuine enthusiasm. This bottled-up energy can lead to increased stress and decreased motivation.

2. Missed Opportunities for Connection: Open communication is the cornerstone of strong relationships. When men hold back their emotions, they may miss opportunities to build trust and rapport with colleagues, ultimately hindering collaboration and team dynamics.

3. Emotional Labor and Burnout: Constantly suppressing emotions can be emotionally draining. This emotional labor can lead to burnout, impacting a man's physical and mental well-being, as well as his work performance.

Navigating Hierarchical Structures

Hierarchical organizational structures can pose challenges for men when expressing vulnerability. In many workplaces, there's a perception that vulnerability is a sign of weakness, especially for those in leadership positions. Men may fear that showing vulnerability could undermine their authority or lead to being viewed as incompetent. This fear can inhibit honest communication and hinder meaningful connections with colleagues.

This dynamic can stifle open communication and hinder innovation.

Here's a closer look at the challenges:

- Power Dynamics: The traditional power imbalance in hierarchical structures can make men feel hesitant to challenge the status quo or express dissenting opinions, even if they have valuable insights to share.

- Fear of Undermining Authority: Openly expressing emotions, particularly frustration or doubt, might be seen as a sign of weakness or a lack of confidence in leadership.

- Limited Role Models: The lack of prominent male leaders who openly express a full range of emotions can create a sense of isolation for men navigating these challenges.

Despite the challenges, there are ways for men to navigate the emotional landscape of the workplace more effectively:

- Challenge the Narrative: Recognize and challenge the limiting stereotypes around masculinity. True strength lies in emotional intelligence, not stoicism.

- Find Your Voice: Practice expressing your emotions in a controlled and professional way. Start small, perhaps with a trusted colleague, and gradually build confidence in expressing yourself authentically.

- Seek Out Allies: Build a network of colleagues who value open communication and emotional intelligence. Having a support system can create a safe space for you to express yourself and navigate challenges.

Remember, leaders who can connect with their teams on an emotional level are seen as more inspiring and effective.

The Impact of Emotional Intelligence on Career Success

Emotional intelligence isn't just about managing your own emotions; it's about understanding and navigating the emotions of others. This skillset is essential for building strong relationships, a key factor in career advancement.

Here's how emotional intelligence empowers you on your professional journey:

- Stronger Networking: People are drawn to those who make them feel valued and understood. Emotional intelligence allows you to build rapport with colleagues and create a network of support that can open doors to new opportunities.

- Effective Communication: Clear and concise communication is crucial for success in any role. Emotional intelligence equips you to express your ideas persuasively, actively listen to others, and navigate difficult conversations with diplomacy.

- Teamwork and Collaboration: The modern workplace thrives on collaboration. Emotional intelligence allows you to work effectively within teams, manage conflict constructively, and inspire others to achieve common goals.

- Adaptability and Resilience: The ability to adapt to change and bounce back from setbacks is essential for long-term success. Emotional intelligence equips you to manage stress effectively, stay motivated, and persevere through challenges.

Leadership Lessons: The Power of Emotional Intelligence in Action

Perhaps the most significant impact of emotional intelligence lies in its power to shape effective leadership. Leaders with high EQ are not just competent; they inspire and motivate their teams.

Here are some key characteristics of emotionally intelligent leaders:

- Self-Awareness: Emotionally intelligent leaders understand their own strengths and weaknesses, allowing them to make informed decisions and lead with authenticity.

- Empathy: These leaders can put themselves in the shoes of their team members, fostering trust and creating a positive work environment.

- Motivation: They can inspire their teams to achieve their full potential by creating a shared vision and fostering a sense of purpose.

- Emotional Regulation: They can manage their emotions effectively, remaining calm and collected under pressure, which provides a sense of stability for their team.

Leading with Empathy: The Power of Emotional Intelligence in Leadership

In today's workplace, strong leadership is more than just barking orders. Effective leaders are those who can inspire, motivate, and unite their teams towards a common goal. This is where emotional intelligence takes center stage.

Here's how emotional intelligence fosters effective leadership:

- Building Trust and Psychological Safety: Leaders with high EQ create a safe space where team members feel comfortable sharing ideas, taking risks, and admitting mistakes. This fosters trust, innovation, and a sense of belonging within the team.

- Conflict Resolution: Teams inevitably face disagreements. Emotionally intelligent leaders can navigate conflict constructively, focusing on solutions rather than blame. This preserves morale and keeps the team moving forward.

- Motivating and Inspiring: Leaders with high EQ can understand the emotional needs of their team members and tailor their leadership style accordingly. They can inspire their teams to achieve great things.

A study by the Hay Group found that emotionally intelligent leaders are:

- 33% more effective at developing their people

- 27% more likely to be rated as high performers by their peers

- 17% more likely to have satisfied customers

These statistics highlight the undeniable impact of emotional intelligence on leadership effectiveness.

Strategies for Navigating the Workplace Dilemma

Emotional intelligence isn't a fixed trait; it's a skill that can be developed. Organizations that invest in emotional intelligence training programs reap significant benefits. These programs equip employees with the tools to:

- Identify Emotions: Recognize their own emotions and the emotions of others, both verbally and nonverbally.

- Understand Triggers: Pinpoint the situations or behaviors that trigger specific emotions.

- Manage Emotions Effectively: Develop healthy coping mechanisms to regulate their emotions in a constructive way.

- Empathize with Others: See things from another person's perspective and build stronger relationships.

- Communicate Effectively: Express their emotions clearly and professionally, fostering open communication.

The impact of emotional intelligence training is far-reaching. Organizations with emotionally intelligent employees experience:

- Increased Employee Engagement: Employees feel valued and invested in their work, leading to higher productivity and job satisfaction.

- Improved Conflict Resolution: EQ fosters constructive communication, allowing teams to address disagreements effectively.

- Enhanced Customer Service: Employees with strong emotional intelligence skills can build rapport with clients and provide exceptional service.

- Reduced Absenteeism and Turnover: A positive work environment, fostered by emotional intelligence, leads to a more stable and committed workforce.

Finding the Right Balance: Authenticity and Professionalism

Emotional intelligence isn't about becoming a walking emotional rollercoaster. It's about striking a balance between expressing yourself authentically and maintaining professionalism.

Here are some tips to achieve this balance:

- Choose Your Battles: Not every situation requires a full-blown emotional response. Learn to discern when it's appropriate to express your emotions and when it's best to take a breath and respond calmly.

- Express Yourself Constructively: Focus on communicating your feelings in a clear and professional manner. Instead of saying "I'm angry," try saying "I feel frustrated when..." and explain the reason behind your emotions.

- Consider the Context: The appropriate way to express your emotions will vary depending on the situation and the people you're interacting with. Use your judgment to determine the most professional way to communicate your feelings.

- Practice Makes Progress: Just like any other skill, emotional intelligence takes practice. Start by incorporating these strategies into your daily interactions, and gradually build your confidence.

- Seek Feedback: Ask trusted colleagues for feedback on your communication style. This can help you identify areas for improvement and ensure your emotional expression is being received as intended.

- Lead by Example: If you're in a leadership position, model emotionally intelligent behavior. By openly expressing your emotions appropriately, you can create a culture where emotional intelligence is valued and encouraged.

Key Takeaways

- Traditional workplaces discouraged emotional expression, hindering communication and collaboration.

- The tide is turning: Modern workplaces value emotional intelligence (EQ) for leadership and team success.

- Men face challenges expressing emotions: Stigmas, hierarchies, and communication styles can create barriers.

- EQ fuels career advancement: Effective communication, strong relationships, and emotional self-management are key.

- Leaders with high EQ are more effective: They build trust, inspire teams, and navigate conflict constructively.

- Emotional intelligence training equips you with skills: Identify emotions, manage them effectively, and build empathy.

- Balance authenticity and professionalism: Express your feelings clearly and constructively in a work-appropriate manner.

- Build a support network: Find colleagues who value open communication and emotional intelligence.

- Leaders who embrace EQ foster a positive work environment: Increased productivity, innovation, and employee satisfaction.

- Invest in your EQ: It's a crucial skill for navigating challenges, building a fulfilling career, and becoming a successful leader.

Now that you've gained insight into how to apply emotional intelligence at work, it's time to consider situations where emotions have impacted you at work. How could emotional intelligence have helped? Explore emotional intelligence training offered by your company or online platforms. Start small. Express your feelings clearly and professionally in a safe space with a trusted colleague. Seek out colleagues who value open communication and emotional intelligence.

Take the next step towards becoming an emotionally intelligent leader by proceeding to the next chapter. Explore practical strategies and insights to elevate your leadership skills and create a positive impact in your professional and personal lives.

Chapter 6: Emotional Leadership

Emotional leadership is a concept that emphasizes the importance of leaders being able to understand and manage their own emotions, as well as recognize and influence the emotions of those around them. It's based on the idea of emotional intelligence, which includes skills such as empathy, self-awareness, and the ability to manage relationships judiciously and empathetically.

Emotional leadership revolves around the ability of leaders to understand, regulate, and leverage emotions effectively. Leaders who excel in emotional intelligence can create a positive work environment, build strong teams, and navigate challenging situations with finesse.

This chapter dives deep into the transformative world of emotional leadership. We will discuss how EQ helps leaders. It shapes team dynamics positively. It fosters a culture of collaboration and trust. Inspiring profiles, practical strategies, and actionable steps will equip you to become an emotionally intelligent leader. This will help you ignite your team's potential.

Embark on a leadership journey where emotional intelligence is your most powerful tool.

Leadership styles have evolved dramatically over time. The stern, top-down commander is being replaced by a nuanced approach. This approach acknowledges the power of emotions. This is where emotional leadership takes center stage.

Emotional Leadership Defined: More Than Just Authority

Emotional leadership goes beyond simply giving orders and expecting results. Harness emotional intelligence (EQ) to create a positive work environment. This boosts productivity. Daniel Goleman, a pioneer in the field of EQ, defines emotional leadership as "the capacity of a leader to recognize their own emotions and those of their people and to use this awareness to motivate, empower, and develop their employees."

Emotional leadership involves building strong relationships with team members. Understanding their needs and motivations is crucial. Creating a safe space for them to express themselves is essential. This builds trust, belonging, and boosts engagement and performance.

The Benefits of Emotional Leadership: A Ripple Effect

The impact of emotional leadership extends far beyond the individual leader. Studies by the Center for Creative Leadership (CCL) show that emotionally intelligent leaders create teams with several key advantages:

- Increased Collaboration: Emotional leaders build trust by fostering psychological safety. Team members can share ideas openly and collaborate effectively toward a common goal.

- Enhanced Innovation: When team members feel comfortable expressing their thoughts and ideas, even unconventional ones, creativity flourishes in such an environment. Emotional leadership fosters this open environment, leading to more innovative solutions.

- Improved Conflict Resolution: Emotional intelligence empowers leaders to navigate conflict constructively. Leaders focus on solutions, not blame. This minimizes disruption and keeps the team moving forward.

- Reduced Stress and Burnout: A positive and supportive work environment is key to employee well-being. Emotional leadership helps create this environment, leading to reduced stress and burnout among team members.

Emotional leadership is not about being overly emotional or sentimental. It's about using your emotional intelligence to create a work environment where everyone feels valued, respected, and empowered to do their best work.

Integrating Emotional Intelligence into Leadership

Leadership styles are categorized in various ways. Some common models focus on decision-making authority or task orientation. However, emotional leadership adds a new dimension to this understanding. Let's explore how different leadership styles can be viewed through the lens of emotional intelligence:

Authoritative Leadership: This style is characterized by a clear vision, decisive action, and the ability to inspire confidence. When combined with high emotional intelligence, authoritative leaders excel at:

1. Communicating the vision with passion and clarity – They inspire team members to believe in the bigger picture and understand their role in achieving it.

2. Building trust through transparency and emotional honesty – Open communication fosters a sense of security and encourages team members to buy into the leader's vision.

3. Providing constructive feedback and fostering development – Emotionally intelligent leaders offer feedback with empathy and focus on growth, motivating team members to reach their full potential.

Democratic Leadership: This style emphasizes collaboration and participation in decision-making. Emotional intelligence is key for democratic leaders to:

1. Create a safe space for open communication. Team members need to feel comfortable expressing ideas without fear of judgment, fostering a sense of psychological safety.

2. Actively listen and acknowledge diverse perspectives. Leaders with high EQ show genuine interest in their team members' thoughts and feelings, fostering a sense of inclusion.

3. Guide the decision-making process effectively. While encouraging participation, emotionally intelligent leaders can ensure discussions stay focused and lead to clear decisions.

Coaching Leadership: This style focuses on developing individuals and maximizing their potential. Emotional intelligence empowers coaches to:

1. Build strong relationships based on trust and empathy. Understanding their team members' strengths and weaknesses allows them to provide personalized coaching and support.

2. Set challenging but achievable goals. Leaders with high EQ can motivate team members by setting goals that are both ambitious and attainable.

3. Provide constructive feedback and celebrate successes. Effective coaching involves offering specific and actionable feedback, delivered in a way that encourages growth. Equally important is recognizing and celebrating achievements, which boosts morale and motivation.

Affiliative Leadership: This style prioritizes harmony and building strong relationships within the team. Emotional intelligence is crucial for affiliative leaders to:

1. Create a positive and supportive work environment. Leaders with high EQ foster a sense of belonging and connection within the team.

2. Recognize and appreciate individual contributions. Feeling valued motivates team members and fosters a spirit of collaboration.

3. Manage conflict constructively. Emotional intelligence allows leaders to navigate disagreements effectively, focusing on solutions rather than blame.

Pacesetting Leadership: This style focuses on setting high standards and driving results. Emotional intelligence helps pacesetting leaders to:

1. Lead by example – Demonstrating a strong work ethic and commitment to excellence inspires team members to strive for their best.

2. Provide clear expectations and performance metrics. Knowing what's expected and how success is measured keeps teams focused and motivated.

3. Recognize and reward high performance. Acknowledging achievement reinforces positive behaviors and motivates continued excellence.

It's important to remember that these leadership styles are not mutually exclusive. Effective leaders often utilize a blend of styles, adapting their approach based on the situation and the needs of their team. Emotional intelligence empowers them to do this effectively, fostering a dynamic and high-performing team environment.

Strategies for Integrating Emotional Intelligence into Leadership

Emotional intelligence involves recognizing others' emotions and understanding your own. Effective emotional leadership hinges on two crucial pillars: self-awareness and self-regulation. These skills empower you to build strong relationships. They also help you lead with empathy.

Knowing Yourself: The Power of Self-Awareness

Self-awareness is the foundation of emotional intelligence. It involves understanding your emotions, their triggers, and their impact on your behaviour. As a leader, this awareness allows you to:

1. Recognize your strengths and weaknesses: Knowing your limitations allows you to delegate tasks effectively and seek support when needed. It also helps you capitalize on your strengths to inspire and motivate your team.

2. Identify emotional triggers: Certain situations or personalities might evoke strong emotions in you. Recognize triggers to manage reactions and respond thoughtfully, not impulsively.

3. Communicate: When you understand your own emotions, you can express them genuinely. This fosters trust and transparency with your team members.

Mastering Your Emotions: The Art of Self-Regulation

Self-regulation is the ability to manage your emotions effectively. It's not about suppressing emotions, but rather about learning to express them in a constructive manner. As an emotionally intelligent leader, you can:

1. Stay calm under pressure: Maintaining your composure during challenging situations allows you to make clear

decisions and offer support to your team. This fosters a sense of security and trust.

2. Manage conflict constructively: When disagreements arise, self-regulation allows you to approach the situation calmly, focusing on solutions rather than assigning blame.

3. Lead by example: Demonstrating emotional control sets a positive tone for your team. When team members see their leader manage stress effectively, they're more likely to adopt similar behaviors.

Leading with Empathy

Empathy is the cornerstone of emotional intelligence and leadership. It goes beyond simply acknowledging someone's emotions; it's about truly understanding their perspective and feelings. By leading with empathy, you can:

1. Build stronger relationships: When team members feel understood and valued, they're more likely to be engaged and motivated.

2. Make more inclusive decisions: Considering different perspectives allows for more informed decision-making that benefits the entire team.

3. Foster a supportive work environment: Empathy allows you to create a space where team members feel comfortable sharing concerns and seeking help.

Tania Singer, a researcher at the University of California, Berkeley, found that empathy activates brain regions linked to compassion and caregiving. This neurological response can foster a sense of trust and cooperation, essential for building a thriving team.

Developing Your Empathy Muscle

Empathy, like other aspects of emotional intelligence, can be developed. Here are some tips:

1. Practice active listening: Pay close attention to both verbal and nonverbal cues when someone is communicating.

2. Put yourself in their shoes: Try to see things from their perspective and understand their challenges.

Ask open-ended questions: Encourage open communication and allow team members to express their feelings.

3. By prioritizing self-awareness, self-regulation, and empathy, you lay the foundation for emotionally intelligent leadership. These skills empower you to build trust, foster collaboration, and create a work environment where everyone feels valued and empowered to do their best work.

Integrating Empathy into Decision-Making

Leaders often make decisions that impact the lives of their team members. Incorporating empathy improves decision-making. It creates a supportive, inclusive workplace.

Here are some tips:

1. Gather Diverse Perspectives: Don't make decisions in a vacuum. Seek input from your team members and consider the potential impact of your choices on everyone involved.

2. Consider the Emotional Impact: Think beyond the practical implications of your decisions. How might they affect the morale, stress levels, and well-being of your team?

3. Communicate Clearly and Openly: Explain your decisions and the reasoning behind them. Be open to feedback and willing to adjust your course if necessary.

Balancing Vulnerability and Authority

Balancing vulnerability and authority as a leader means being strong and compassionate. This involves being decisive and empathetic.

Emotional leadership thrives on trust. Team members trust their leader. They feel safe expressing themselves, taking risks, and collaborating effectively. This trust is built through transparency – the willingness to share information openly and honestly.

Vulnerability: Not Weakness, But Strength

Leadership has been associated with strength and infallibility. However, emotional leadership flips this script. Being vulnerable, such as admitting mistakes or sharing personal experiences, helps you create a more human connection with your team. This vulnerability fosters trust and encourages others to be open and honest as well.

The University of California, Berkeley study found that teams rated leaders showing vulnerability as more competent and effective. This highlights the power of vulnerability in building trust and fostering a positive work environment.

Putting Transparency and Vulnerability into Practice

1. Admit Mistakes: Don't shy away from owning up to errors in judgment. Acknowledge your mistakes and explain the lessons learned. This shows your team that you're human and allows them to learn from your experiences.

2. Share Information Openly: Keep your team informed about project developments, challenges, and even setbacks. This transparency fosters trust and empowers them to contribute effectively.

3. Celebrate Wins (and Learn from Losses): Acknowledge and celebrate successes with your team. Equally important, be open about setbacks and use them as learning opportunities. This shows authenticity and encourages your team to learn from both positive and negative experiences.

The Ripple Effect of Emotional Leadership: Shaping a Positive Workplace Culture

Emotional leadership doesn't exist in a vacuum. When leaders cultivate self-awareness, empathy, and navigate vulnerability effectively, it creates a ripple effect impacting the entire team and organizational culture.

- Increased Psychological Safety: By fostering trust and openness, emotional leadership creates a space where team members feel safe to take risks and share ideas without fear of judgment. This psychological safety is crucial for innovation and high performance [2].

- Enhanced Collaboration: When team members trust and respect each other, collaboration becomes more natural. Open communication and a shared sense of purpose pave the way for effective teamwork.

- Improved Employee Engagement: Emotional leadership fosters a more positive and supportive work environment, leading to increased employee engagement and reduced turnover. Employees who feel valued and appreciated are more likely to be invested in their work.

- A Culture of Continuous Learning: Transparency and vulnerability allow for open feedback and facilitate a culture of continuous learning. Mistakes become learning experiences, and team members are encouraged to grow and develop their skills.

Emotional leadership isn't about micromanaging emotions or creating a space of emotional chaos. It's about striking a balance between authority and vulnerability, fostering a positive work environment, and empowering your team to achieve great things.

By cultivating emotional intelligence and utilizing the strategies outlined in this chapter, you can become a leader who inspires trust, ignites creativity, and builds a thriving team culture.

Cultivating Emotional Leadership in Your Team

Leadership Self-Assessment: Begin by reflecting on your leadership style. What are your strengths? Where do you see opportunities for growth? Delve into your emotional intelligence, evaluating how well you understand and manage your own emotions, as well as those of others. Use tools like self-reflection journals or leadership assessment surveys to gain insights into your leadership approach.

Team Collaboration Challenge: Now, it's time to put your insights into action. Propose a challenge within your team that focuses on implementing emotional intelligence practices. Encourage open communication, active listening, and empathy. Foster an environment where team members feel comfortable expressing their emotions and opinions. Track the impact of these initiatives on collaboration, productivity, and overall team dynamics. Remember, true leadership isn't about commanding from the top—it's about empowering others to shine and thrive collaboratively. Take the first step towards becoming the emotionally intelligent leader your team deserves.

Key Takeaways

- Understand the essence and importance of emotional leadership in shaping organizational dynamics.

- Demonstrate the practical techniques for infusing emotional intelligence into your leadership style, enhancing team performance and cohesion.

- Master the balance between vulnerability and authority, fostering trust and respect within your team.

- Recognize the profound influence of emotional leadership on organizational culture, driving positivity and productivity.

- Embrace your role as an agent of change, empowered to cultivate a positive work environment through emotional intelligence.

- Reflect on your leadership style, identifying strengths and areas for growth in emotional intelligence.

- Propose initiatives within your team to implement emotional intelligence practices, fostering collaboration and growth.

- Embrace a lifelong journey of learning and development in emotional leadership, recognizing its transformative potential.

- Take solid steps to integrate emotional intelligence into your leadership approach, catalyzing positive change and fostering a culture of empowerment.

Embrace the transformative power of emotional leadership. Start implementing these steps today. Cultivate a positive work environment and empower your team for success.

Reflect on your emotional intelligence strengths and growth areas using the self-assessment tool. Challenge your team to practice active listening and witness the power of empathetic communication.

Chapter 7: Nurturing Collaborative Workspaces

The modern workplace thrives on collaboration. Teams that function cohesively achieve more, solve problems efficiently, and foster a sense of shared purpose. The American Psychological Association states that a collaborative team is likely to see a 24% increase in innovation. Additionally, they may experience a 33% improvement in problem-solving skills and increased job satisfaction.

A cohesive team uses diverse perspectives, encourages innovation, and faces challenges directly. Here, vulnerability is not a weakness but a catalyst for growth.

This chapter explores how effective communication creates collaborative workspaces.

Effective communication goes beyond simply conveying information. It acknowledges feelings, fosters empathy, and creates a safe space for open communication.

This chapter explores how collaborative environments impact productivity. This chapter gives you strategies to improve communication. It helps your team work better together.

Understanding the Role of Effective Communication in Teamwork

Communication is the lifeblood of teamwork. It allows team members to share ideas, solve problems, and work towards a common goal. But effective communication goes beyond simply conveying information.

Effective teamwork goes beyond simply exchanging information. It's a dynamic dance that considers both the what and the how of communication. Traditional communication focuses on the message itself: the facts, figures, and instructions. Emotional communication, however, acknowledges the emotional undercurrents that influence how messages are received and interpreted.

Here's how effective communication influences teamwork:

1. Building Trust: Clear and open communication fosters trust within the team. When team members feel their voices are heard and their ideas valued, they're more likely to collaborate effectively.

2. Enhancing Understanding: Effective communication encourages team members to consider diverse perspectives and gain a deeper understanding of the issues at hand. This fosters a more collaborative and inclusive work environment.

3. Promoting Active Listening: Effective communication requires active listening, where you truly focus on understanding the speaker's message, both verbal and nonverbal. This builds trust and ensures everyone feels heard and valued.

4. Navigating Conflict Constructively: Disagreements are inevitable in any team. Effective communication allows for conflict to be addressed constructively, focusing on finding solutions rather than assigning blame.

Research backs the positive impact of collaborative work environments. The American Psychological Association study found that effective teams enjoy various benefits, such as:

1. Increased Innovation: Collaboration fosters a cross-pollination of ideas, leading to more creative and innovative solutions.

2. Enhanced Problem-Solving: Diverse perspectives within a team allow for a more comprehensive understanding of challenges and the development of more effective solutions.

3. Improved Job Satisfaction: Feeling valued, supported, and heard within a collaborative team contributes to increased job satisfaction and motivation.

4. Boosted Productivity: When team members work together effectively, communication is streamlined, tasks are delegated efficiently, and overall productivity increases.

Collaboration achieves results. It fosters belonging and a shared purpose. Team members who openly express themselves create a positive work experience. Team members who work together towards a common goal also contribute to this positive experience. This experience is rewarding. Collaboration motivates individuals and teams, making the workforce more engaged and productive.

Practical Tips for Effective Communication

Now that we understand the power of effective communication, let's explore some practical tips for integrating it into your daily interactions:

1. Clarity is Key: Present information clearly, concisely, and in a way that is easy for everyone to understand. Avoid jargon and technical terms whenever possible.

2. Embrace Transparency: Share information openly and honestly, fostering trust within the team. Explain the reasoning behind decisions and keep everyone informed about progress.

3. Pay Attention: Being attentive to both verbal and nonverbal cues, and ask clarifying questions to ensure understanding. Put away distractions and make eye contact to show you're fully engaged.

4. Emphasize Empathy: Try to see things from the other person's perspective and acknowledge their feelings. A simple phrase like "It sounds like you're concerned about..." can go a long way.

5. Encourage Two-Way Communication: Create a space where everyone feels comfortable sharing their ideas and feedback. This fosters a more collaborative and inclusive environment.

By incorporating these practices, you can create a foundation for effective communication that empowers your team to collaborate effectively and achieve remarkable results.

Challenges in Fostering Effective Communication at Work

We've established the power of effective communication in fostering a collaborative and successful team environment. But truly, clear and open communication doesn't always happen naturally in the workplace. As effective communication is the cornerstone of successful teamwork, there can be challenges that hinder effective communication in workplaces.

Communication Barriers

1. Fear of Judgment: A major barrier is the fear of being criticized or appearing incompetent. Studies by the University of California, Berkeley, show that this fear can lead to employees withholding valuable ideas and hindering innovation. Creating a safe space for open dialogue and acknowledging the value of diverse perspectives is crucial to overcoming this barrier.

2. Lack of Trust: Without trust, collaboration crumbles. A study published in Harvard Business Review highlights the connection between trust and effective communication within teams. Building trust takes time and requires consistent effort. Leaders who demonstrate transparency, keep their promises, and value team members' input foster a foundation of trust.

3. Misunderstandings: Nonverbal cues, cultural differences, and communication styles can all lead to misunderstandings. Research by the International Journal of Business Communication emphasizes the importance of clear and concise communication, coupled with active listening, to bridge these gaps.

4. Information Overload: In today's fast-paced work environment, information overload is a real concern. A study by the American Psychological Association reveals that constant emails, messages, and meetings can make it difficult to focus on and absorb important information. Prioritizing communication channels, setting clear expectations for response times, and encouraging focused meetings can help alleviate information overload.

5. Conflicting Communication Styles: We all have preferred communication styles; some are direct and concise, while others are more indirect and nuanced. A study by Personality and Social Psychology Bulletin suggests that recognizing these differences and adapting your communication style accordingly can improve understanding and collaboration.

Building the Bridge to Collaboration

So, how do we overcome these challenges and build a culture of effective communication? Here are some evidence-based strategies:

1. Be an Example: Leaders set the tone for the team culture. By demonstrating effective communication skills—active listening, clear communication, and empathy—leaders create a model for others to follow. Research by Gallup highlights the link between strong leadership communication and employee engagement.

2. Invest in Team Building: Well-designed team-building activities can be powerful tools for fostering trust, communication, and collaboration. A study published in the International Journal of Business and Management found that team-building activities that encourage teamwork on challenging tasks or promote shared laughter can break down barriers and build stronger bonds within the team.

3. Embrace Transparency: Open and honest communication builds trust. Share information about company goals, project updates, and decision-making processes with the team. A study by the Society for Human Resource Management highlights the importance of transparency in building trust and fostering a positive work environment.

4. Provide Training: Invest in communication skills training for your team. This can help team members develop their active listening skills, assertive communication techniques, and

conflict resolution strategies. Research by the American Society for Training and Development shows that communication skills training can lead to improved teamwork and overall job performance.

Creating a Culture of Emotional Support

Collaboration thrives in an environment where team members feel not just valued for their skills, but also supported on a human level.

Leadership Influence

Leaders play a pivotal role in fostering a culture of emotional support. Their actions and behaviors set the tone for the entire team. Here's how effective leaders cultivate this vital aspect of collaboration:

1. Leading by Example: Leaders who embody emotional intelligence demonstrate empathy, active listening, and open communication. It has been found that leaders who display emotional intelligence foster trust and psychological safety within their teams, leading to increased innovation and collaboration.

2. Promoting Open Communication: Leaders who promote open communication create a space for team members to comfortably share ideas, concerns, and frustrations. Holding

regular team meetings with open agendas, actively soliciting feedback, and practicing active listening are ways leaders can achieve this. The Society for Human Resource Management (SHRM) research confirms open communication drives employee engagement and job satisfaction.

3. Building Trust: Trust is the foundation of any strong team. Leaders can build trust by being transparent, keeping their promises, and acknowledging team members' contributions. A meta-analysis published in the Journal of Applied Psychology found a strong correlation between trust and team performance.

4. Celebrating Achievements—Big and Small: Recognition goes a long way in fostering a supportive environment. Leaders can celebrate both individual and team achievements, big or small. This reinforces positive behaviors and motivates team members to continue contributing their best work. Research by the Achievers Workforce Institute highlights the link between employee recognition and increased engagement, productivity, and retention.

5. Providing Constructive Feedback: Leaders who provide constructive feedback, focused on behavior and offering specific suggestions for improvement, empower their team members to learn and grow. A study published in the Harvard Business Review emphasizes the importance of creating a "growth mindset" within teams, where challenges are seen as opportunities for development.

These leadership actions create a safe space for team members to be themselves, openly express their emotions, and collaborate effectively.

Team-Building Exercises: Cultivating the Soil of Collaboration

Team-building exercises are more than just a fun office activity. When strategically chosen, they can be powerful tools for fostering trust, empathy, and open communication—the essential ingredients for emotional support. Here are some effective exercises:

1. Strengths-Based Activities: These activities help team members identify and appreciate each other's strengths. One simple exercise involves having each team member write down their top three strengths and then sharing them with the group. This fosters understanding and appreciation for the unique value each person brings to the team.

2. Shared Challenges: Exercises that involve working together to overcome a common challenge can be a powerful way to build trust and communication. Escape room challenges or collaborative problem-solving activities encourage teamwork and communication in a fun and engaging setting.

3. Volunteer Activities: Giving back to the community through volunteer work can be a rewarding experience that strengthens team bonds. Working together towards a common goal outside the traditional work environment fosters empathy and understanding. A study by the Corporation for National

Service found that volunteerism can lead to increased collaboration and communication skills within teams.

4. Open Communication Games: Games that encourage open communication and active listening can help team members feel more comfortable expressing themselves. One example is "Two Truths and a Lie," where each team member shares three statements, two of which are true and one is a lie. The others have to guess which statement is the lie. This lighthearted activity can help break down communication barriers and encourage team members to listen attentively.

By prioritizing emotional support through strong leadership and strategic team-building exercises, you cultivate an environment where individuals feel valued, heard, and empowered. This collaborative ecosystem allows diverse perspectives to flourish, fostering creativity, innovation, and ultimately, remarkable results. The next section dives deeper into the specific strategies team members can adopt to foster emotional support within their teams. We'll explore communication techniques, conflict resolution approaches, and the power of active listening to build a truly collaborative team.

The Pillars of Individual EQ

Emotional intelligence equips you with the skills to navigate team dynamics effectively. Here's how you can leverage your EQ to contribute to a high-functioning team:

- Self-Awareness: This involves understanding your emotions, how they influence your thoughts and actions, and how you perceive yourself. Self-aware team members can recognize their strengths and weaknesses, and adjust their behavior accordingly to contribute effectively in different situations.

- Self-Regulation: This refers to your ability to manage your emotions effectively. Emotionally intelligent team members can manage stress, control impulses, and stay calm under pressure. This allows them to navigate challenging situations constructively and avoid letting emotions cloud their judgment.

- Social Awareness: This is the ability to understand the emotions, needs, and perspectives of others. Socially aware team members can empathize with colleagues, build rapport, and foster a sense of trust and connection within the team.

- Relationship Management: This involves building and maintaining positive relationships. Emotionally intelligent team members communicate effectively, handle conflict constructively, and collaborate effectively with others.

- Motivation: This refers to your intrinsic drive to achieve goals. Highly motivated team members are passionate about their work and inspire others with their enthusiasm.

Emotional Intelligence for Conflict Resolution

Disagreements are inevitable in any team setting. But for high-performing teams, conflict becomes an opportunity for growth and innovation, not a roadblock to progress. Emotional intelligence (EQ) plays a crucial role in navigating these situations constructively.

Here are some strategies that leverage emotional intelligence for effective conflict resolution:

1. Self-Management: The Art of Staying Calm

Emotional intelligence isn't just about understanding others' emotions; it's also about managing your own. During conflict, self-management is critical. Techniques like deep breathing, taking a short break, or mentally reframing the situation can help you approach the conversation with a cooler head. By managing your own emotions, you can avoid escalating the situation and create a space for productive dialogue.

2. Empathy: Stepping into Another's Shoes

A core component of emotional intelligence is empathy—the ability to understand and share the feelings of another person. In conflict resolution, empathy allows you to see the situation from your teammate's perspective. Actively listen to their concerns, acknowledge their feelings, and validate their point of view. This fosters trust and creates a collaborative environment where solutions can be found.

3. Communication: Finding Common Ground

Clear and concise communication is essential for resolving conflict. Express your own feelings and needs. Focus on the issue at hand, avoiding personal attacks or blame games. By communicating effectively, you can bridge the gap between perspectives and find common ground.

Building a Culture of Mutual Respect

By integrating these emotional intelligence strategies, teams can transform conflict from a disruptive force into a catalyst for growth. Remember, fostering a culture of mutual respect is key. Treat each other with respect, even during disagreements. This allows for open communication, honest feedback, and ultimately, a stronger, more collaborative team.

Putting EQ into Action

Here are some practical strategies to integrate emotional intelligence into your daily team interactions:

- Active Listening: Give your full attention to your team members when they speak. Understand the person's message, ask clarifying questions if needed, and avoid interrupting. This demonstrates respect and encourages open communication.

- Empathy in Action: Put yourself in your colleagues' shoes. Try to understand their perspectives and challenges.

Phrases like "It sounds like you're concerned about X" show empathy and build trust.

- Positive Communication: Be expressive about your needs and concerns. Avoid accusatory language and focus on finding solutions. Positive communication fosters collaboration and reduces defensiveness.

- Celebrate Diverse Perspectives: Don't shy away from expressing your ideas, but also appreciate the value of different viewpoints. Ask questions to understand differing opinions and explore how they can strengthen the team's approach.

This chapter equips you, the conductor, with the tools to cultivate emotional intelligence within your team, leading them towards a collaborative masterpiece.

Tuning In: Diagnosing Your Team's EQ

It is imperative to have a thorough understanding of your subordinate's present situation before assuming leadership.

Here's a diagnostic approach to assessing your team's emotional intelligence:

Step 1:

Pay attention to team meetings. Are discussions dominated by a few voices? Do emotions run high, hindering progress? These steps might indicate a lack of self-awareness or social awareness within the team.

Step 2:

Observe team dynamics. Do members work well together or exhibit solo acts? A prevalence of solo acts might suggest challenges with relationship management or a lack of shared motivation.

Step 3:

Analyze project outcomes. Does the team consistently miss deadlines or fail to meet goals? Poor performance could be a sign of underlying emotional intelligence issues impacting collaboration and overall effectiveness.

Once you've diagnosed your team's EQ strengths and weaknesses, it's time to conduct them towards a collaborative masterpiece.

Here are some actionable steps:

The Self-Awareness Exercises

Encourage team members to reflect on their strengths and weaknesses through personality quizzes or journaling exercises. This self-awareness is the foundation for individual and collective emotional intelligence.

The Emotional Intelligence Training

Invest in workshops on emotional intelligence and conflict resolution. Equip your team with the tools to manage emotions, navigate interpersonal challenges, and build stronger relationships.

Your Role

As the leader, embody emotional intelligence. Practice active listening, acknowledge emotions, and manage conflict constructively. Your actions set the tone for the entire team.

1. Foster open and honest communication by creating a safe space for team members to share ideas and concerns. Hold regular meetings with clear agendas that encourage active participation from all members.

2. Celebrate the unique perspectives and experiences each team member brings to the table. Encourage respectful dialogue and value the power of diverse viewpoints in fostering innovation.

3. Build an environment of safety where team members feel safe to take risks, share ideas, and admit mistakes. Encourage experimentation, acknowledge effort, and celebrate learning from mistakes.

4. Recognize and appreciate team members who display emotional intelligence in their interactions with others. Public recognition or incentive programs can reinforce the importance of these skills.

5. Organize team-building activities that promote trust, communication, and collaboration. Consider activities that encourage teamwork on challenging tasks or promote shared laughter and camaraderie.

Developing emotional intelligence as a team is an ongoing process. Consistently implement these strategies. Create a culture fostering collaboration. Empower individuals. Allow your team to perform at its peak. Embrace the journey, and together, create a collaborative symphony that surpasses all expectations.

Key Takeaways

- Emotional communication significantly influences teamwork dynamics, fostering trust and cohesion among team members.

- Addressing common barriers to emotional communication, such as fear of vulnerability, is essential for cultivating a collaborative workspace.

- Effective leadership plays a pivotal role in creating a culture of emotional support and collaboration within teams.

- Embrace the unique perspectives and experiences each team member brings to the table. A variety of viewpoints fuels creativity and innovation.

- Create an environment where team members feel safe to take risks, share ideas, and admit mistakes without fear of punishment. This psychological safety fosters trust and collaboration.

- Open and honest communication is the cornerstone of collaborative workspaces. When team members feel safe to share ideas and concerns, innovation flourishes, and problems are solved more effectively.

- Disagreements are inevitable, but with emotional intelligence, they can become opportunities for growth. By managing emotions, practicing empathy, and focusing on solutions, teams can navigate conflict productively.

We've seen how emotional intelligence builds successful team harmony. Remember, a collaborative team requires consistent effort, open communication, and a commitment to fostering emotional well-being.

The next chapter delves into a crucial aspect of emotional intelligence – individual awareness. We'll explore the concept of traditional masculinity and its impact on emotional expression. The chapter explores how ingrained stereotypes affect relationships, personal development, and societal expectations. Gain insights to challenge outdated norms and promote inclusivity and authenticity. These strategies are practical and valuable for all aspects of life.

Part 3: Shaping a Stronger Identity through Sensitivity

Chapter 8: Deconstructing Traditional Masculinity

In a world where societal norms often dictate gender roles and expectations, the concept of masculinity has long been confined to a narrow and rigid definition. However, as we evolve as a society, it becomes increasingly apparent that these traditional notions of masculinity are not only outdated but have done more harm than good.

This chapter challenges traditional masculinity. The journey is thought-provoking. By examining the societal constructs that have shaped our understanding of what it means to be a man, we aim to pave the way for a more authentic and inclusive identity. It's time to question the stereotypes, stigmas, and expectations placed upon men and to embrace a broader spectrum of masculinity—one that celebrates diversity, vulnerability, and emotional authenticity. This exploration empowers individuals to break free from traditional masculinity. It helps them embrace a more liberated sense of self. Delve into masculinity complexities.

Analyzing the Limitations of Conventional Masculinity

Societal Expectations

Boys are taught traditional masculinity traits like strength, stoicism, and dominance from a young age. Society expects men to follow norms. These are reinforced by media, peer pressure, and stereotypes. Pressure to conform can create a rigid framework. It restricts men from exploring their identity. Men can't express themselves authentically. Men who closely follow traditional masculine norms are more prone to mental health problems like depression, anxiety, and substance abuse.

Impact on Emotional Expression

The pressure to conform to traditional masculinity can have a profound impact on a man's emotional well-being in several ways.

When boys are discouraged from expressing a full range of emotions, they develop a limited emotional vocabulary. This makes it difficult for them to identify and communicate their feelings effectively, leading to frustration and misunderstandings in relationships. Imagine trying to navigate a complex situation with only a handful of words to describe your internal state.

Difficulty with Vulnerability: Traditional masculinity often equates vulnerability with weakness. This makes it challenging for men to open up about their struggles, seek support, or build deep, emotionally intimate connections. Without vulnerability, relationships can become superficial and lack the trust and understanding needed to truly thrive.

The "Man Box": The concept of the "man box" refers to the narrow range of emotions and behaviors deemed acceptable for men. This box can be stifling, preventing men from exploring their full potential and expressing themselves authentically. It's like being forced to wear a suit that's several sizes too small; it restricts movement and hinders your ability to function at your best.

The Cost of Emotional Suppression

The impact of adhering to traditional masculinity goes beyond just emotional well-being. Here's a look at the toll conventional masculinity, which often discourages emotional expression, can take on men's well-being:

- Mental Health Burdens: Studies show men are less likely to seek help for mental health issues. Bottling emotions can lead to anxiety, depression, and even physical health problems.

- Strained Relationships: Difficulty expressing emotions can create distance in relationships. Partners may feel disconnected or unheard, leading to conflict and dissatisfaction.

- **Fatherhood Impediments:** Emotional suppression can hinder a father's ability to connect with his children. Children need dads who can validate their feelings and model healthy emotional expression.

- **Missed Opportunities for Growth:** Suppressing emotions limits your ability to learn and grow. By opening up about challenges and failures, you can gain valuable insights and build resilience.

- **A Life Half-Lived:** Living in fear of expressing emotions can rob you of a fulfilling life. Vulnerability allows you to experience joy, love, and connection more deeply.

By breaking free from the constraints of traditional masculinity, men can cultivate greater emotional resilience, healthier relationships, and a more authentic sense of self. It's time to liberate ourselves from outdated gender norms and embrace a more inclusive and compassionate vision of masculinity.

Challenging Conventional Beliefs

Men should be able to express their emotions freely, pursue interests traditionally deemed "feminine," and prioritize mental well-being without facing social stigma. Men experience emotions just as intensely as women do. Yet, societal norms dictate that they suppress these feelings. Why? Because vulnerability is seen as weakness, true strength lies in acknowledging our emotions, not in bottling them up. When we allow ourselves to feel, we become more authentic and more human.

Men who defy the stoic stereotype often suffer in silence. They grapple with anxiety, depression, and loneliness, afraid to seek help. Why? Because admitting vulnerability feels like a betrayal of their masculinity. But it's time to rewrite the script.

Questioning What You Believe

Masculinity isn't monolithic. It's a spectrum that encompasses a diverse range of emotions, behaviours, and interests. Yet, stereotypes paint a narrow picture: men are stoic, emotionless, and aggressive. But are these truly the only facets of masculinity? Here's how to challenge these ingrained beliefs:

- Interrogate Your Assumptions: Reflect on your own beliefs about masculinity. Where did they come from? Are they based on societal expectations or your personal values? Challenge any limiting stereotypes you hold about yourself or other men.

- Expand Your Horizons: Seek out positive portrayals of men who defy traditional masculinity. Look for books, movies, and TV shows that feature male characters who express a full range of emotions and interests.

- The Power of "And": Masculinity doesn't have to be an "either/or" proposition. You can be strong and compassionate, assertive and nurturing. Embrace the concept of "and" to create a more holistic definition of masculinity that aligns with your values.

The Stigma Factor: Breaking Down the Barriers

Men who deviate from traditional masculinity often face social stigma. They may be labeled as "weak," "effeminate," or "not a real man." This stigma can be isolating and discourage men from expressing themselves authentically. Here's why dismantling the stigma is crucial:

- The Cost of Conformity: Conforming to unrealistic expectations can lead to a disconnect from one's authentic self. This can have a negative impact on mental health and overall well-being.

- Silencing Vulnerability: The stigma against emotional expression prevents men from seeking help when they need it. Creating a space for open communication about emotions is vital for men's mental health.

- A Missed Opportunity for Connection: When men feel pressured to conform, they miss out on the richness of human connection that comes from authentic expression.

Building a More Accepting World: Practical Steps

We can all play a role in dismantling the stigma surrounding non-traditional masculinity. Here are some ways to contribute:

- Challenge Sexist Jokes and Comments: Don't let sexist jokes or comments go unchecked. Speak up and challenge these harmful stereotypes.

- Celebrate Diversity: Actively celebrate men who defy traditional masculinity. Let them know their authentic expression is valued and appreciated.

- Lead by Example: Embrace your own emotional vulnerability and challenge traditional gender roles in your own life. This sets a positive example for others.

Embracing Authenticity: The Power of Being You

Moving beyond stereotypes opens the door to a more fulfilling experience of masculinity. Here's what you gain by embracing your authentic self:

- Improved Mental Health: Expressing emotions in a healthy way can reduce stress, anxiety, and depression.

- Stronger Relationships: Being vulnerable allows you to build deeper, more meaningful connections with others.

- A Life Lived on Your Terms: When you break free from societal expectations, you can live a life that aligns with your values and aspirations.

Encouraging Authentic Self-Expression

Strength Beyond the Stereotype

The traditional view of masculinity depicts men as emotionless and strong. While emotional control and resilience are certainly valuable traits, this narrow definition excludes a vast spectrum of what it means to be a man.

Here's why celebrating this diversity is crucial:

Strength Comes in Many Forms: Physical strength is just one facet of masculinity. Emotional intelligence, compassion, and vulnerability are equally important qualities. Embracing diverse expressions helps men become well-rounded individuals. They can navigate life's complexities with a broader skillset.

Beyond the Binary: Masculinity doesn't exist in opposition to femininity. It exists on a spectrum, allowing men to incorporate traditionally "feminine" traits like nurturing and creativity into their identity. This broader definition fosters a more inclusive vision of masculinity that allows all men to feel like they belong.

Breaking Free from Limitations: The limitations of traditional masculinity can hinder personal growth. Embracing diverse expressions allows men to explore different interests and activities, leading to a more fulfilling life. A man enjoys rock climbing and tending to his garden. Both activities can boost self-esteem and well-being through diverse expressions of masculinity.

The Benefits of Diversity in Masculinity

Studies have shown a clear link between embracing diverse expressions of masculinity and positive outcomes for men. In 2018, the Journal of Counseling Psychology published a study. It found that men with flexible masculinity views had better self-esteem and life satisfaction. Additionally, a 2020 study in the Psychology of Men and Masculinity found that men who felt comfortable expressing a wider range of emotions had stronger social relationships.

Impact on Mental Health

The restrictive nature of traditional masculinity can have a profound impact on men's mental health.

- Emotional Suppression and its Toll: Discouraging men from expressing a full range of emotions leads to emotional suppression. This can manifest as stress, anxiety, and difficulty coping with challenges. Unexpressed emotions don't disappear; they fester and can lead to outbursts of anger or difficulty managing emotions in healthy ways.

- Be a Loner: The image of the self-sufficient, independent man can be isolating. It discourages men from seeking help or building strong support networks, hindering their emotional well-being. Men who struggle to connect and share their burdens are more susceptible to feelings of loneliness and depression.

- The Pressure to Conform: The pressure to conform to a narrow definition of masculinity can create immense internal conflict. Men who feel they don't measure up to the stereotype may experience feelings of inadequacy and shame, further impacting their mental health.

Promoting Emotional Resilience

Building Emotional Resilience

Traditional masculinity discourages men from acknowledging and processing emotions. This leads to a lack of emotional resilience. Men can develop emotional resilience and cope with life's challenges by breaking free from constraints. One effective strategy is to practice mindfulness and emotional awareness. Men can deepen their self-understanding by being attentive to thoughts and feelings without judgment.

Another crucial aspect of building emotional resilience is developing healthy coping mechanisms. Instead of resorting to harmful behaviors like substance abuse or aggression to numb their emotions, men can explore constructive outlets such as journaling, exercise, or engaging in hobbies they enjoy. These activities not only provide a healthy release for pent-up emotions but also promote overall well-being.

Seeking professional help through therapy or counseling can be immensely beneficial. A trained therapist can provide guidance and support in navigating complex emotions, offering tools and techniques to enhance emotional resilience. Participating in support groups or men's circles can create a sense of community and validation. This normalizes the experience of emotional vulnerability.

Empowering Vulnerability

Contrary to the belief that vulnerability is a sign of weakness, embracing vulnerability can actually contribute to emotional strength and well-being. When men allow themselves to be vulnerable, they create authentic connections with others and foster deeper intimacy in their relationships.

To empower vulnerability, men can start by challenging the societal norms that equate vulnerability with weakness. Instead, they can reframe vulnerability as an act of courage and authenticity. By sharing their thoughts, feelings, and struggles with trusted friends or partners, men can cultivate a sense of belonging and support that bolsters their emotional resilience.

Practicing self-compassion is essential to embracing vulnerability. Men should learn to treat themselves with kindness and understanding, especially during times of distress or failure. By embracing their imperfections and acknowledging their humanity, men can develop a stronger sense of self-worth and resilience in the face of adversity.

In summary, promoting emotional resilience involves breaking free from the constraints of traditional masculinity and embracing vulnerability as a source of strength. By cultivating emotional awareness, healthy coping mechanisms, and self-compassion, men can build the resilience needed to navigate life's challenges with grace and authenticity.

Some inspiring journeys of individuals who have deconstructed traditional masculinity and embraced a more authentic way of being highlight the positive outcomes of this transformation.

From Wrestler to Therapist: The Evolution of Glenn Stanton

Glenn Stanton was once known as "Stone Cold" Steve Austin, a larger-than-life professional wrestler. His on-screen persona embodied the traditional image of masculinity – tough, aggressive, and stoic. However, after retiring from wrestling, Stanton embarked on a surprising journey. He returned to school to become a therapist; a profession often stereotyped as "feminine." This career shift sparked criticism, but Stanton remained undeterred. In an interview with The Guardian, he stated, "Being a man isn't about how tough you are... It's about being there for people, being present, and being vulnerable." Stanton's journey exemplifies the power of breaking free from stereotypes and pursuing a path that aligns with one's values.

It's inspiring to see someone challenge societal norms and embrace a different path, regardless of expectations. Stanton's journey reminds us that true strength lies in compassion, empathy, and authenticity.

From Football Field to Fashion Icon: The Duality of Harry Styles

Harry Styles, a former member of the boy band One Direction, has become a cultural icon known for his flamboyant fashion sense and emotional vulnerability. He regularly challenges traditional notions of masculinity by wearing clothing typically associated with women, such as dresses and high heels. Despite criticism, Styles remains unapologetically himself. In a 2020 interview with Vogue, he stated, "What's feminine isn't weak and what's masculine isn't strong." Styles' success demonstrates that embracing a more fluid and expressive form of masculinity can be commercially viable and culturally impactful.

From Boardroom to Ballroom: The Artistic Expression of Derek Hough

Derek Hough, a multiple-time champion on the dance competition show "Dancing with the Stars," is another example of a man defying stereotypes. In a world where dance is often seen as a feminine pursuit, Hough excels in a traditionally "feminine" art form while maintaining a strong and confident presence. His artistry and dedication have earned him immense respect and popularity. Hough's story highlights the importance of embracing diverse passions and celebrating artistic expression, regardless of gender norms.

Key Takeaways

- Traditional masculinity norms often constrain men's emotional expression, limiting their ability to fully engage with their feelings and experiences.

- Embracing a broader definition of masculinity challenges stereotypes and fosters emotional well-being, leading to healthier and more fulfilling relationships.

- Recognizing vulnerability as a strength rather than a weakness empowers men to cultivate emotional resilience and navigate life's challenges with authenticity and courage.

- Breaking free from rigid gender expectations allows men to explore and celebrate their unique identities, fostering a sense of self-acceptance and belonging.

- Society's narrow definition of masculinity can contribute to mental health issues such as depression and anxiety, highlighting the importance of promoting diverse expressions of gender identity.

- Encouraging open dialogue about masculinity helps dismantle harmful stereotypes and promotes a culture of acceptance and inclusivity.

- Individuals who challenge traditional masculinity norms often experience greater personal growth and fulfillment as they embrace their authentic selves.

- Building emotional intelligence enables men to cultivate healthier relationships and communicate effectively with others, enriching both personal and professional interactions.

- Embracing vulnerability fosters empathy and compassion, strengthening connections with others and creating a more empathetic society.

- By deconstructing traditional masculinity, men can lead more fulfilling lives, free from the constraints of outdated gender norms, and contribute to a more equitable and inclusive world.

Deconstructing traditional masculinity means breaking free from societal constraints. It also involves embracing authenticity and promoting emotional well-being. Challenging gender norms and celebrating diverse expressions of masculinity can help individuals develop self-awareness, resilience, and compassion. Embracing vulnerability as strength requires courage and self-reflection. The benefits are deeper connections, healthier relationships, and personal fulfillment.

We will continue to explore masculinity further in the next chapter. It will focus on embracing sensitivity as a strength, not a weakness. You will discover how sensitivity can be a source of resilience, empathy, and authentic connection.

Chapter 9: Strength in Sensitivity

In a world where strength is often synonymous with physical prowess or unyielding resilience, it's time to challenge these conventional notions and redefine strength within the realm of emotional vulnerability.

Embracing sensitivity isn't about succumbing to fragility; rather, it's about showing emotions that make us uniquely human.

When we embrace our sensitivity, we open ourselves up to deeper connections with others, fostering empathy, understanding, and compassion. This heightened emotional awareness strengthens our interpersonal relationships.

Embracing sensitivity empowers us to navigate life's complexities with grace and resilience. Rather than viewing sensitivity as a liability, we recognize it as a superpower—an invaluable tool for self-discovery, personal growth, and navigating the world with empathy and compassion.

Strength isn't just about enduring hardships with a stiff upper lip; it's about having the courage to confront our emotions openly and authentically.

True strength lies in our ability to acknowledge our vulnerabilities and face them head-on. It's the courage to express our fears, insecurities, and doubts, even when society tells us to suppress them. By embracing our emotional vulnerability, we demonstrate an unparalleled strength of character—the strength to be true to ourselves, despite the pressures to conform to societal norms.

It takes immense strength to empathize with others, to lend a listening ear, and to offer support in times of need. This kind of strength isn't measured by physical might but by the depth of our compassion and empathy.

Redefining strength in emotional vulnerability empowers us to embrace humanity fully. We believe real strength comes from embracing emotions fully. It's okay to be vulnerable because vulnerability is a powerful strength.

Through this chapter, we'll explore the several ways in which embracing sensitivity can lead to greater fulfilment, resilience, and overall well-being

The Mindset Shift

To find strength in sensitivity, a transformative mindset shift is essential. Traditionally, sensitivity has been stigmatized as a weakness, often associated with vulnerability and fragility. However, to unlock its true potential, men must reframe their perception of sensitivity and recognize it as a profound source of strength.

For many men, sensitivity feels like a double-edged sword. It fosters emotional connections and empathy. However, it may trigger self-doubt and a fear of appearing weak.

The first step towards embracing your sensitivity is to challenge the narrative you've been conditioned to believe. Society often portrays sensitivity as a feminine quality, contrasting it with the supposed "strength" of stoicism.

One effective strategy for shifting our mindset is practicing self-compassion. By treating ourselves with kindness and understanding, we can break free from self-judgment and embrace our sensitivity with greater acceptance.

Men often suppress emotions and conform to stereotypes of toughness and stoicism. By questioning these norms and embracing a more inclusive definition of masculinity, individuals can liberate themselves from the constraints of societal expectations.

It is essential to recognize the inherent value of sensitivity in fostering deeper connections and empathy.

Sensitivity helps individuals understand emotions, fostering better relationships and boosting emotional intelligence. Rather than viewing sensitivity as a liability, men can reframe it as a superpower that enriches their lives and empowers them to navigate the complexities of the human experience with grace and authenticity.

By engaging in mindfulness meditation, individuals can develop a greater awareness of their thoughts and emotions, allowing them to observe without judgment. Self-reflection encourages individuals to examine their beliefs and behaviours, challenging internalized stigma and fostering self-acceptance.

Embracing sensitivity as a source of strength requires courage and vulnerability. It involves stepping into discomfort, dismantling ingrained beliefs, and redefining personal identity. Embarking on this journey unlocks sensitivity's power. Men gain resilience, authenticity, and emotional well-being.

Building Confidence in Expressing Sensitivity

Building confidence in expressing sensitivity requires courage and self-assurance. One powerful approach is to start small by gradually exposing ourselves to situations where we can express our emotions authentically. This might involve sharing our feelings with trusted friends or loved ones, writing in a journal, or engaging in creative outlets such as art or music.

Setting boundaries and advocating for our emotional needs are crucial to building confidence. It's essential to communicate assertively and assertively communicate our boundaries to others, allowing us to honor our emotional well-being while fostering genuine connections.

Research indicates that individuals who embrace their sensitivity and express their emotions authentically experience greater psychological well-being and resilience. By reshaping our personal identity to view sensitivity as a strength and building confidence in expressing it, we empower ourselves to lead more fulfilling and authentic lives. Through this chapter, we'll explore additional strategies for harnessing the power of sensitivity to cultivate resilience, deepen connections, and thrive in a world that celebrates authenticity.

Here are examples of men who have defied stereotypes and discovered immense strength by embracing their sensitivity.

Vulnerability on the Court: Kevin Love, a star athlete in the NBA, shattered traditional expectations by openly discussing his struggles with anxiety and depression. Love's vulnerability resonated with millions, demonstrating that strength lies not in suppressing emotions, but in acknowledging and dealing with them head-on. His courage to share his story inspired countless men to seek help for their own mental health struggles, proving that emotional intelligence and vulnerability are not signs of weakness, but essential tools for a fulfilling life.

Leading with Empathy: Howard Schultz, former CEO of Starbucks, attributes his success to his ability to connect with his employees on an emotional level. Schultz prioritizes empathy and emotional intelligence in leadership, creating a company culture that values open communication and vulnerability. His approach challenges the stereotype of the cold, emotionless CEO, proving that strong leadership thrives on compassion and understanding.

The Artist's Raw Emotion: John Mayer, a Grammy-winning singer-songwriter, pours his heart and soul into his music. His lyrics explore a range of emotions, from vulnerability and heartbreak to joy and love. Mayer's willingness to express his emotions authentically resonates deeply with fans, proving that sensitivity is not a hindrance to artistic expression, but a powerful source of inspiration.

From Warrior to Healer: Russell Wilson, a star quarterback in the NFL, embodies the evolving definition of masculinity. Beyond his athletic prowess, Wilson is known for his compassion and emotional intelligence. He actively supports mental health initiatives and speaks openly about his faith, challenging the stereotype of the tough, emotionless athlete. Wilson's vulnerability inspires fans and demonstrates that strength comes in many forms, including the courage to be open and caring.

These are just a few examples of men who have redefined strength. Their stories challenge the misconception that sensitivity is a weakness. Instead, they demonstrate that embracing your emotions can lead to deeper connections, greater self-awareness, and ultimately, a richer and more fulfilling life.

Self-Care Practices

Self-care practices play a pivotal role in enhancing emotional well-being, particularly for men who embrace sensitivity. By prioritizing self-care, men can nurture their emotional health and embark on a journey of self-discovery that celebrates their sensitivity rather than viewing it as a weakness.

1. Mindfulness Meditation: Engaging in mindfulness meditation allows men to cultivate present-moment awareness and develop a deeper connection with their thoughts and emotions. Through regular practice, individuals can learn to observe their feelings without judgment, fostering self-acceptance and emotional resilience.

2. Journaling: Journaling provides a constructive outlet for men to explore their thoughts and emotions in a safe and private space. By putting pen to paper, individuals can gain insight into their innermost feelings, identify patterns of behaviour, and track their emotional journey over time. Journaling can serve as a powerful tool for self-reflection and self-expression.

3. Creative Expression: Engaging in creative activities such as writing, painting, or playing music can be highly therapeutic for sensitive men. These outlets allow individuals to channel their emotions into artistic expression, providing a sense of catharsis and empowerment. Through creative endeavours, men can tap into their innermost feelings and express them in meaningful and authentic ways.

4. Nature Walks: Spending time in nature offers a respite from the stresses of daily life and allows men to reconnect with their surroundings and themselves. Whether it's a stroll through the woods or a hike in the mountains, immersing oneself in nature can promote relaxation, reduce anxiety, and enhance overall well-being. Nature serves as a powerful healer, providing solace and perspective to sensitive individuals seeking refuge from the pressures of modern society.

4. Physical Exercise: Engaging in regular physical exercise not only benefits one's physical health but also has profound effects on emotional well-being. Activities such as jogging, yoga, or weightlifting release endorphins—natural mood lifters—and reduce stress hormones, promoting a sense of calm and balance. Exercise offers a constructive way for sensitive men to channel their energy and emotions, improving both their physical and mental health.

In essence, self-care practices provide sensitive men with the tools they need to navigate their emotional landscape with confidence and resilience. By embracing mindfulness, journaling, creative expression, spending time in nature, and prioritizing physical exercise, men can embark on a journey of self-discovery that celebrates their sensitivity and promotes emotional well-being.

Unveiling Your Strengths: A Personal Journey of Discovery

Embracing sensitivity isn't just about recognizing its value; it's also about understanding how it manifests uniquely within each individual. As we embark on this journey of self-discovery, let's delve into the empowering process of conducting a strengths inventory to unveil the hidden treasures within our sensitivity.

1. Understanding Your Emotional Landscape: Begin by reflecting on your emotional responses to various situations. What emotions do you frequently experience, and how do they influence your actions and interactions? By identifying your emotional triggers and patterns, you gain valuable insight into your emotional landscape.

2. Recognizing Patterns of Sensitivity: Explore recurring themes in your life where sensitivity plays a significant role. Are there specific contexts or environments where you feel most attuned to your emotions? Pay attention to moments when your sensitivity serves as a guiding compass, leading you towards deeper connections and insights.

3. Identifying Strengths in Vulnerability: Challenge the misconception that vulnerability equates to weakness. Instead, recognize vulnerability as a profound strength—one that allows you to connect authentically with others and cultivate meaningful relationships. Your ability to empathize, communicate openly, and navigate complex emotions is a testament to your inner strength.

4. Embracing Authenticity: Authenticity lies at the heart of genuine social engagement. Encourage yourself to show up authentically in your interactions, expressing your sensitivity without fear of judgment or rejection. By embracing your true self, you create space for meaningful connections and foster a sense of belonging.

5. Setting Boundaries: Remember that authenticity doesn't mean sacrificing your well-being. Set boundaries that honour your needs and protect your emotional energy. Communicate assertively and respectfully; assert your limits when necessary, prioritizing self-care and emotional resilience.

6. Embracing Growth: View your sensitivity as a source of continual growth and self-discovery. Embrace new experiences, challenges, and opportunities for personal development. As you navigate life's journey, remember that every obstacle is an opportunity for growth and empowerment.

7. Celebrating Your Sensitivity: Finally, celebrate your sensitivity as a unique and invaluable aspect of your identity. Embrace the richness of your emotional landscape, recognizing that your sensitivity is not a flaw to be corrected but a strength to be celebrated.

Through this strengths inventory, you'll gain a deeper understanding of your sensitivity and the unique strengths it brings to your life

Key Takeaways

- Redefining Strength: Sensitivity isn't a weakness, it's a sign of emotional intelligence, a crucial predictor of success in life. Embrace your vulnerability as a source of strength.

- Mindset Shift: Challenge the inner critic that labels sensitivity as "unmanly." Reframe sensitivity as a strength and recognize the positive aspects like empathy, deeper connection, and emotional awareness.

- Building Confidence: Express your sensitivity with confidence. Start small in low-pressure situations, practice assertive communication, and celebrate your victories in expressing your authentic self.

- Self-Compassion and Mindfulness: Treat yourself with kindness and understanding. Use mindfulness techniques to observe your thoughts and emotions without judgment, fostering self-compassion and authentic communication.

- Self-Care Practices: Sensitivity can guide your self-care journey. Pay attention to your needs and personalize your self-care practices with activities like meditation, spending time in nature, or creative expression.

- Building Support Networks: Surround yourself with people who create a safe space for vulnerability. Supportive relationships provide a sense of belonging, foster empathy, and combat feelings of isolation.

- Strengths Inventory: Identify your unique strengths associated with sensitivity. Empathy, intuition, and emotional intelligence are valuable assets. Create a living document to track your growth and celebrate your strengths.

- Authentic Social Engagement: Start small and gradually express your sensitivity in social settings. Lead by example, focus on quality connections, and embrace the imperfections that come with vulnerability.

This chapter has been a transformative journey into the power of embracing your sensitivity. You've learned to reframe your mindset, build confidence in expressing yourself, and navigate the world with greater emotional intelligence. Remember, sensitivity isn't a weakness; it's a superpower waiting to be unleashed.

In the next chapter, we'll explore the evolving roles and expectations of fathers in today's society, challenging traditional stereotypes and embracing a more inclusive and nurturing approach to parenting.

Chapter 10: Redefining Fatherhood

My dad wasn't a man of many words, especially about emotions. He was a rock, a steady presence in my life, but expressing feelings wasn't his forte. I became a father myself, and I realized something – I wanted to be different. Sure, I wanted to provide for my kids, be their steady hand, but I also craved a deeper connection. So, I started small. Sharing my excitement at their successes began with tiny victories. The unrestrained whoop when my son finally mastered his bike, a sheepish confession of exhaustion during a marathon diaper change, and yes, even a glistening tear during that animated film about the lost puppy (you know the one). The initial awkwardness, the fear of seeming "unmanly," slowly dissolved. In its place bloomed a garden of genuine connection. My children saw me not just as Dad, but as a whole person, comfortable with the full spectrum of emotions. I shared my excitement at their successes, openly expressing my frustration during a particularly trying bedtime routine. Gone are the days when being a father merely meant providing for the family—a stoic figure shielding loved ones from life's storms. Today, fatherhood transcends these roles, weaving emotional threads that bind families together. Emotional vulnerability emerges as a cornerstone of this transformation. Fathers now recognize that strength lies not only in physical prowess but also in the courage to express feelings openly. The once-impenetrable armour cracks, revealing a tender heart eager to connect with children on a profound level.

This chapter reveals how parent-child relationships transform, emphasizing fathers' key role in shaping family emotions. By challenging outdated stereotypes and embracing authenticity, fathers are forging new paths, fostering environments where emotional expression thrives.

Emotional Vulnerability within Parenting

Dads – the grill masters, the joke tellers, and the unshakeable pillars of support. That's the image that's been ingrained in society for generations. The truth is, the role of fathers is undergoing a beautiful transformation. We're shifting from the stoic stereotype. We're embracing a new model of fatherhood. It's based on emotional intelligence and vulnerability. This might sound counterintuitive, but here's the thing: expressing your emotions isn't a sign of being "soft" on your kids; it's actually a power move that benefits everyone involved.

Dads no longer bear sole responsibility for providing food and discipline. Today, fathers are actively involved in every aspect of their children's lives – from diaper changes to bedtime stories. This shift isn't just practical; it recognizes fathers' impact on children's emotional well-being.

Modern fathers are encouraged to connect emotionally with their children by sharing feelings and vulnerabilities. Research in developmental psychology has consistently shown that children benefit greatly from having emotionally engaged fathers. When fathers are actively involved in their children's lives and provide emotional support, children exhibit higher levels of self-esteem, empathy, and social competence.

Research backs this up. A study published in the Journal of Family Psychology found that children raised by involved fathers experience a range of positive outcomes, including:

- Stronger emotional intelligence: Dads who openly express and manage their emotions create a safe space for their children to do the same. This translates into better self-awareness, empathy, and social skills for kids.

- Improved communication skills: By talking openly about their feelings, fathers' model healthy communication habits for their children. This sets them up for success in building strong relationships throughout their lives.

- Enhanced self-esteem: A father's love and emotional support act as a powerful confidence booster for children. Knowing they have someone they can rely on emotionally fosters a sense of security and self-worth.

The Science of Connection

So, how exactly does a father's emotional vulnerability translate into positive outcomes for children? Here's where the science gets interesting.

Studies by the University of California, Berkeley, have shown that children raised by emotionally engaged fathers have a stronger prefrontal cortex, the part of the brain responsible for emotional regulation, decision-making, and impulse control. In simpler terms, dads who express their emotions are helping their children develop the ability to navigate their own emotional world effectively.

But the benefits extend beyond brain development. Emotional connection creates a sense of security and trust between fathers and children. Imagine your son struggling with a bully at school. Bottling up his emotions could lead to feelings of isolation and helplessness. However, if he feels comfortable opening up to you, expressing his fear and anger, you can offer support, guidance, and a safe space to process his emotions. This fosters resilience, reduces stress, and strengthens the father-child bond.

The Power of Vulnerability in Everyday Moments

Embracing emotional vulnerability doesn't require grand gestures. It starts with the little things – celebrating your daughter's artwork with genuine excitement, admitting you're feeling overwhelmed during a particularly chaotic bedtime routine, or simply sharing a laugh during a movie night.

These everyday moments of emotional connection send a powerful message to your children: "It's okay to feel your emotions, and it's okay to express them." This creates a safe space for your children to explore their own emotional landscape without fear of judgment.

Emotionally engaged fathers play a crucial role in fostering resilience and coping skills in their children. By modeling healthy emotional expression and coping mechanisms, fathers can help their children navigate life's challenges with confidence and resilience. Studies have shown that children with emotionally available fathers are better equipped to regulate their emotions, cope with stress, and form secure attachments with others.

Redefining fatherhood isn't about abandoning tradition; it's about enriching it. By embracing your emotional intelligence and fostering meaningful connections with your children, you're not just being a dad – you're becoming a role model, a confidant, and a source of unwavering support.

Strategies for Emotionally Supportive Parenting

Effective communication skills are the cornerstone of emotionally supportive parenting. As fathers, our ability to communicate openly and effectively with our children lays the foundation for fostering emotional openness and resilience. But what does effective communication entail?

1. Mastering the Art of Communication:

Communication is the lifeblood of any relationship, and the father-child bond is no exception. Here's the good news: you don't need a psychology degree to be a communication whiz. Here are some practical tips to foster emotional openness with your kids:

- Become an Active Listener: This goes beyond simply hearing the words your child is saying. Active listening involves giving your full attention, making eye contact, and acknowledging their feelings. When our children speak, we must listen attentively, without judgment or interruption. This demonstrates that their thoughts and feelings are valued, encouraging them to express themselves freely

- Validate Their Emotions: Ever feel dismissed as a kid when you were told to "stop crying" or "it's not a big deal"? Don't perpetuate that cycle. Let your children know their feelings are valid, even if you don't necessarily agree with the source of those emotions. Say things like, "I see you're feeling frustrated," or "It's okay to be scared." Validating your children's emotions doesn't mean agreeing with everything they say, but rather acknowledging and accepting their feelings as valid and understandable. This builds trust and strengthens the parent-child bond.

- Use "I" Statements: This helps avoid blame games and promotes understanding. Instead of saying, "You always make such a mess!" try, "I feel frustrated when toys are left on the floor." This shifts the focus to how their actions impact you, encouraging them to consider your perspective.

- Embrace Open-Ended Questions: "Yes or no" answers won't get you very far. Ask questions that encourage your child to elaborate on their feelings, like "What happened that made you so angry?" or "Tell me more about how you're feeling."

2. Emotional Transparency

Think back to your childhood. Do you remember a time your dad expressed his sadness or frustration in a healthy way? Perhaps it was a heartfelt conversation after a loss, or a moment of vulnerability during a challenging project. These instances, where dads model emotional expression, have a profound impact on children.

Here's how to make emotional transparency a part of your fatherhood journey:

- Normalize the Full Spectrum of Emotions: Let your kids see you experience joy, excitement, sadness, anger, and everything in between. Don't shy away from expressing frustration when necessary.

- Embrace the "Ugly Cry" Moment: We all get sad sometimes, dads included. Don't be afraid to let your children see you tear up during a touching movie scene, or share your worries about the future. This shows them it's okay to feel sad, and that vulnerability is a sign of strength, not weakness.

- Own Your Mistakes and Apologize: We're all humans, and messing up is inevitable. When you make a mistake, be open about it and apologize to your children. This teaches them accountability and the importance of emotional repair in relationships.

- Celebrate Each Other's Victories (Big and Small): Jumping for joy after your son scores his first goal is a no-brainer, but what about acknowledging his progress in mastering his multiplication tables? Let your children see your genuine excitement for their achievements, no matter how big or small.

Moreover, creating a safe space for emotional expression is paramount. Fathers should establish an environment where their children feel comfortable sharing their feelings without fear of judgment or ridicule. Encourage open dialogue, validate their emotions, and reassure them that they are loved unconditionally.

Navigating Traditional Expectations and Pressures

Embracing emotional vulnerability can feel like breaking the mold. One of the primary challenges of traditional fatherhood lies in the deeply ingrained societal expectations placed on men. From a young age, boys are socialized to suppress their emotions, leading to a reluctance to express vulnerability or seek support when needed. This can create a barrier for fathers who wish to forge deeper emotional connections with their children but feel constrained by societal norms.

Let's explore the challenges of breaking away from the stereotype and equip you with strategies to become the emotionally supportive dad you (and your kids) deserve to be.

The Challenge: Redefining Fatherhood

Imagine this scenario: you're playing catch with your son. He misses a throw and gets frustrated, kicking the dirt in anger. What's your first instinct? Do you:

A) Crack a joke to lighten the mood?

B) Offer a pep talk about sportsmanship?

C) Acknowledge his frustration and offer support?

The "ideal dad" stereotype might push you towards A or B. But here's the truth – option C is the most emotionally supportive response. Why? Because it validates your son's feelings and shows him it's okay to experience and express frustration.

But acknowledging your child's emotions can feel unnatural, especially if your own father wasn't exactly a model of emotional expression. It's no surprise, then, that many dads face challenges in breaking away from these traditional expectations. Here are some common hurdles:

- The Fear of Seeing "Soft": Society often equates emotional vulnerability with weakness. But here's the secret: expressing your emotions takes strength, not weakness. It's about being authentic and creating a genuine connection with your children.

- The Pressure to be the "Strong One": Dads are often seen as the emotional pillars of the family. While providing stability is important, it's equally crucial to show vulnerability. Your children need to know it's okay to rely on you for emotional support, not just practical needs.

- The "Boys Don't Cry" Mentality: This outdated idea stifles emotional expression in men from a young age. Breaking free allows you to model healthy emotional expression for your sons. This sets them up for success in their own relationships.

Empowering fathers to overcome societal pressures and embrace a more emotionally present and supportive role involves a multifaceted approach that addresses both internal and external factors. Here are some strategies for fathers to consider:

- Self-awareness: Encourage fathers to reflect on their own beliefs and attitudes towards masculinity and fatherhood. By becoming aware of any internalized societal pressures or expectations, fathers can begin to challenge and redefine their roles in alignment with their values and aspirations.

- Open communication: Foster an environment of open communication within the family. Encourage fathers to engage in meaningful conversations with their children, actively listening to their thoughts, feelings, and concerns. By creating space for dialogue, fathers can strengthen their emotional connection with their children and cultivate trust and understanding.

- Seek support: Encourage fathers to seek support from peers, mentors, or mental health professionals. Breaking away from traditional notions of stoicism and seeking help when needed is a sign of strength, not weakness. By sharing their experiences and challenges with others, fathers can gain valuable insights and resources to navigate their parenting journey more effectively.

- Lead by example: Role-modeling emotional openness and vulnerability is crucial for fathers seeking to embrace a more supportive role. Demonstrate the importance of expressing a wide range of emotions authentically and encourage children to do the same. By leading by example, fathers can create a safe and nurturing environment where emotional expression is valued and encouraged.

- Flexible parenting styles: Encourage fathers to adopt flexible and adaptive parenting styles that prioritize emotional connection and responsiveness. Recognize that there is no one-size-fits-all approach to parenting and encourage fathers to tailor their parenting practices to meet the unique needs of their children.

- Challenge gender stereotypes: Encourage fathers to challenge traditional gender stereotypes and embrace a more inclusive and egalitarian approach to parenting. By actively participating in caregiving tasks and sharing household responsibilities, fathers can model gender equality and demonstrate that nurturing and caregiving are not solely the domain of mothers.

Overall, empowering fathers to overcome societal pressures and embrace a more emotionally present and supportive role requires a willingness to challenge traditional norms, cultivate self-awareness, seek support, and prioritize authentic emotional connection with their children.

Building Emotional Connections with Children

Building emotional connections with children is not just about being physical. It also requires meaningful interactions to build emotional bonds. Spending quality time with children strengthens parent-child bonds. It greatly impacts their emotional well-being and development.

Firstly, quality time entails being fully present and attentive when interacting with children. Put away distractions like phones and work thoughts. Focus only on the child. Engage with genuine interest and enthusiasm when playing a game, reading a story, or having a conversation.

Moreover, engaging in activities that promote emotional bonding is essential. These activities can vary depending on the child's interests and age but should ideally involve opportunities for open communication, shared experiences, and mutual enjoyment.

So, what does quality time actually look like? It's not about passively watching TV together (although that can have its place occasionally!).

Here are some ideas to get you started:

- Get Down on Their Level: Literally! Play games, build forts, and read stories together. These activities create a sense of fun and connection, fostering emotional intimacy.

- Embrace Their Interests: Is your daughter obsessed with horses? Take her to a riding lesson, even if horses aren't your thing. Showing genuine interest in their passions demonstrates your love and support.

- Unplug and Be Present: Put away your phone and silence distractions. Being fully present in the moment allows you to truly connect with your children on an emotional level.

- Make Mealtimes Memorable: Dinner can be more than just refueling. Turn it into a conversation starter, asking your children about their day and sharing your own experiences.

- Embrace Bedtime Rituals: Story time, singing lullabies, and even just a few quiet moments of cuddling before sleep foster a sense of security and emotional connection.

Embracing vulnerability is another crucial aspect of building emotional connections with children. Children learn by example, and when fathers demonstrate vulnerability by openly expressing their emotions, it teaches children that it's okay to be vulnerable and authentic. This fosters an environment of trust and openness where children feel comfortable expressing their own emotions without fear of judgment.

Research has shown that children who have emotionally engaged fathers tend to have higher self-esteem, better social skills, and improved academic performance. Additionally, they are less likely to engage in risky behaviors such as substance abuse or delinquency.

In conclusion, building emotional connections with children through quality time and vulnerability not only strengthens the parent-child bond but also lays the groundwork for their emotional and psychological well-being. By prioritizing these aspects of parenting, fathers can cultivate deeper, more meaningful relationships with their children that last a lifetime.

Promoting Co-Parenting Partnerships

Whether through divorce, separation, or blended families, fostering a healthy emotional environment for your children requires a unique approach. Here's the good news: by prioritizing communication and shared emotional responsibility, you can build a strong co-parenting partnership that benefits everyone involved.

Bridging the Gap: The Power of Communication

Communication is the lifeblood of any successful relationship, and co-parenting is no exception. However, in these situations, communication takes on an added layer of complexity. Here are some strategies to cultivate open and effective communication:

- Beyond the "Handoff": Co-parenting communication extends beyond just scheduling logistics. Schedule regular check-ins to discuss your children's emotional well-being, academic progress, and any concerns you may have. These conversations foster collaboration and ensure a united front when it comes to emotional support.

- Respectful Dialogue, Even in Disagreements: Disagreements are inevitable, but avoid turning communication into a battlefield. Focus on respectful dialogue, even when you don't see eye-to-eye. Remember, the goal is to prioritize your children's emotional well-being, not win an argument.

- Be more concerned about your goals: When communication gets heated, remind yourselves why you're doing this—for the emotional and psychological well-being of your children. This shared purpose can help navigate difficult conversations and keep you focused on what truly matters.

Your daughter returns home from school devastated after a fight with a friend. She longs to talk to you but hesitates. She's unsure if your response will be like the one from her other parent. In this kind of scenario, she will mostly prefer to speak to her mom before thinking about her dad.

Presenting a unified approach to emotional support with your co-parent creates security and consistency for your children. They can express themselves freely without fear. Conflicting responses or emotions are not a concern. Here's how to move beyond potential conflict and establish a united front:

- Focus on Shared Goals: Despite potential disagreements, remind yourselves that you both share the same ultimate goal – the emotional well-being of your children. Keeping this "why" at the forefront helps navigate challenging conversations and fosters collaboration.

- Develop a Communication Style: Work with your co-parent to establish a communication style that feels comfortable for both of you. This might involve regular check-ins, utilizing a co-parenting app, or simply agreeing on respectful communication even during disagreements.

- Embrace Transparency: Keep each other informed about your children's emotional state, any concerns you might have, and any upcoming events or milestones. This transparency fosters a sense of partnership and ensures a cohesive approach to emotional support.

Beyond Communication: Sharing the Emotional Load

Communication is crucial, but the real magic happens when you and your co-parent actively share the emotional responsibility of raising your children. Here are some ways to ensure your children feel supported, regardless of where they are:

- Quality Time, No Matter the Distance: Make the most of your time with your children, even if it's limited. Be fully present, actively listen to their concerns, and offer emotional support. Technology can be your friend – utilize video calls to connect when you're apart.

- Consistency is Key: Work with your co-parent to establish consistent routines and expectations regarding emotional support. This might include bedtime rituals, communication norms regarding emotional outbursts, and positive reinforcement strategies.

- Celebrate Milestones Together: Did your son finally conquer his fear of stage fright during the school play? Celebrate his achievement, even if you weren't there in person. Express your pride and acknowledge his effort – this fosters a sense of unity and security.

- Embrace Different Parenting Styles: Acknowledge that you and your co-parent might approach emotional support differently. Focus on finding common ground and respecting each other's parenting style, as long as it creates a safe and nurturing environment for your children.

Key Takeaways

The traditional expectations of fatherhood are evolving. Society is recognizing the importance of emotional connection and vulnerability in dads.

- Emotional Intelligence Matters: Dads who are emotionally intelligent raise children who are better equipped to manage their own emotions and build healthy relationships.

- Breaking Free from the Mold: Challenge societal pressures to conform to a rigid definition of masculinity. Embrace your full emotional range to be a more present and supportive father.

- Quality Time is Key: Invest in quality time with your children, creating a space for open communication and emotional bonding. It's not about the quantity, but the emotional connection you build.

- Vulnerability is Strength: Sharing your emotions with your children models healthy expression and creates a safe space for them to do the same. Don't be afraid to show your tears or laughter.

- Embrace the Full Spectrum: Let your children see you experience joy, sadness, anger, and everything in between. Suppressing emotions sends the wrong message.

- Validate Their Feelings: Acknowledge your children's emotions, even if you don't necessarily agree with the source. Say things like "I see you're feeling frustrated" to show you understand.

- Open Communication is Vital: Talk to your children about their day, their feelings, and their worries. Practice active listening and create a space where they feel comfortable sharing openly.

- Co-Parenting Partnerships Thrive on Communication: Work with your co-parent to establish clear communication and shared emotional responsibility, ensuring a unified front for your children.

- Embrace the Journey: Redefining fatherhood is a continuous process. Reflect on your experiences, celebrate your victories, and seek support when needed. You are not alone on this path.

Redefining fatherhood involves embracing emotional vulnerability, challenging traditional norms, and fostering deeper connections with children. By empowering fathers to embrace their authentic selves, we can create healthier family dynamics and nurture happier, more resilient children.

Conclusion

The Road Ahead

I'm happy that you made it to the end of this book. We explored masculinity deeply in this book. We have uncovered the layers of men's "hidden struggle." You've seen the power of vulnerability in building connections and leading emotionally. You learned emotions, explored workplace dilemmas, and deconstructed traditional masculinity.

We explore emotional vulnerability in men. This challenges conventional beliefs and embraces authenticity. Each chapter guides us to understand ourselves and our relationships better.

Now, you stand on the precipice of this newfound awareness. Imagine a life where:

- **Your partner** feels truly seen and heard. You openly communicate your needs and desires. This builds a deeper connection based on trust and emotional intimacy.

- **Your children** thrive in an emotionally safe space. You model healthy emotional expression. They can navigate feelings confidently.

- **Your workplace** transforms into a collaborative haven. You foster trust, respect, and belonging among your team.

- **You** experience a profound sense of self-acceptance. You embrace all facets of your emotional being, no longer afraid to show the world the authentic you

As we conclude this exploration, let's reflect on the insights gained and the road ahead.

Embracing Vulnerability: Men often suppress feelings due to societal expectations, which causes internal turmoil. This can lead to isolation. We shed light on this silent struggle. This is the first step to breaking free from emotional repression. It's time to liberate ourselves from the shackles of societal expectations and embrace our authentic selves.

The Power of Vulnerability: We explored the transformative power of vulnerability. Embracing vulnerabilities helps us connect deeply with others and be authentic. We have seen how vulnerability sparks personal growth and meaningful relationships through stories and research. Let's remember that true strength is being vulnerable and authentic. It leads to a fulfilling life.

Navigating Relationships: We explored how open communication, empathy, and understanding foster intimate partner connections. Embracing vulnerability in relationships creates trust, intimacy, and support. Let's commit to showing up authentically and vulnerably in our relationships. This will nurture the bonds that enrich our lives.

Mastering Emotional Intelligence: Emotional intelligence is crucial for success at work and in leadership roles. Integrate these principles into our professional lives, creating collaborative environments where everyone thrives.

Masculinity is Redefined: Traditional notions are deconstructed. This paves the way for a more inclusive definition. It is also more compassionate. Let's challenge outdated stereotypes and embrace the diversity of masculine identities.

Fathers can redefine fatherhood by prioritizing emotional connection and support. Let's lead by example, fostering resilience, empathy, and authenticity in the next generation. Armed with knowledge, self-awareness, and empathy, we can navigate life's challenges gracefully. We are equipped to handle difficulties with resilience. Continue building emotional intelligence, practicing self-care, and embracing vulnerability for strength.

Here are ten points encompassing the strategies needed for success:

1. Self-awareness: Understand your emotional landscape and recognize when you're experiencing internal struggles

2. Courage to be vulnerable: Embrace vulnerability as a strength, allowing yourself to authentically express emotions

3. Effective communication skills: Learn to communicate openly and honestly in relationships, fostering understanding and connection.

4. Emotional literacy: Develop the ability to recognize and articulate emotions, enhancing self-awareness and empath.

5. Emotional intelligence in the workplace: Cultivate emotional intelligence to navigate professional challenges and foster collaborative workspaces.

6. Leadership skills: Acquire leadership qualities such as empathy, resilience, and authenticity to inspire and motivate others

7. Creating a supportive environment: Foster psychological safety and trust within teams to encourage collaboration and innovation

8. Challenging societal norms: Challenge traditional notions of masculinity and embrace vulnerability as a source of strength

9. Embracing sensitivity: Recognize the strength found in sensitivity and vulnerability, both personally and in relationships

10. Reimagining fatherhood: Redefine fatherhood by prioritizing emotional connection, support, and authenticity in relationships with children

By incorporating these tools into your life, you can navigate the complexities of emotional vulnerability, foster meaningful relationships, and thrive personally and professionally.

Now is the time to take action. Commit to living authentically. Embrace vulnerability. Champion emotional expression in ourselves and others. Together, we can create a world where sensitivity is celebrated and emotional well-being is prioritized.

As we embark on the road ahead, let's remember that true strength lies in our ability to be vulnerable, to connect deeply with others, and to live authentically. May this journey lead us to a life filled with meaning, fulfillment, and genuine human connection.

Key Takeaways

- Emotional vulnerability is a strength, not a weakness: Throughout the book, we've emphasized that embracing vulnerability allows for authentic connections and personal growth.

- Effective communication is paramount in all relationships: Whether in personal or professional relationships, open and honest communication fosters understanding, trust, and empathy.

- Traditional masculinity is evolving: We've explored the limitations of conventional masculinity and highlighted the importance of redefining societal norms to promote inclusivity and emotional expression.

- Emotional intelligence is essential for success: Cultivating emotional intelligence enables individuals to navigate challenges, lead effectively, and foster collaborative environments.

- Workplaces thrive on collaboration and emotional support: Creating a culture of collaboration and emotional support enhances productivity, innovation, and employee satisfaction.

- Leadership requires emotional authenticity: Effective leadership is grounded in authenticity, empathy, and vulnerability, inspiring trust and motivation in teams.

- Self-awareness is key to personal growth: Understanding and accepting your emotions and vulnerabilities is fundamental to personal development and meaningful relationships.

- Sensitivity is a source of strength: Contrary to societal norms, sensitivity is a strength that fosters deeper connections, empathy, and resilience.

- Fatherhood is about emotional connection, not just provision: Redefining fatherhood involves prioritizing emotional presence, support, and engagement in your children's lives

- Authenticity breeds fulfillment: Ultimately, embracing emotional vulnerability and authenticity leads to more fulfilling relationships, personal well-being, and a more inclusive society.

By internalizing these key takeaways, you can navigate the complexities of emotions, relationships, and societal expectations with greater confidence, resilience, and authenticity.

This book, "Emotional Vulnerability in Men," has provided you with invaluable tools and insights to embrace vulnerability as a source of strength and navigate life's challenges with authenticity.

As we conclude this enlightening journey together, remember that your journey towards emotional growth and self-discovery is ongoing. Embrace each moment as an opportunity for growth and connection.

I believe in you! You have the power to cultivate meaningful relationships, lead with empathy, and live a life filled with purpose and fulfillment.

I hope this book has been helpful to you. If you have any questions or need further support along your journey, please don't hesitate to reach out. I am here to support you every step of the way.

If you found this book helpful and transformative, please consider leaving a review on Amazon. Your feedback will not only inspire others to embark on their own journeys of self-discovery and emotional growth but also motivate us to continue creating meaningful books that empower and uplift.

THANK YOU

Thank you for choosing "Emotional Vulnerability in Men." Your support and interest in this book mean the world to me.

I poured my heart and soul into crafting this guide to provide expert insights and practical strategies to help you uncover your authentic self and achieve personal growth. I hope that you have found the content valuable and empowering.

As an independent author, your feedback and review on the platform where you purchased the book would be immensely valuable. By sharing your thoughts, you help me grow as a writer and also assist others in discovering the transformative power of emotional vulnerability.

Your support fuels my passion for writing and motivates me to continue creating content that resonates with you and addresses your needs.

To leave a review please click below

Richard Garraway Author Page

Thank you for investing in " Emotional Vulnerability in Men."

With heartfelt appreciation,

Richard Garraway

References (Book 2)

Levant, R. F. (2020). The Tough Standard: The Hard Truths About Masculinity and Violence

American Psychological Association (APA). (2021). Speaking of Psychology: Men, masculinity, and mental health, with Ronald F. Levant, EdD2

Daniel Goleman - Emotional Intelligence https://www.amazon.com/Emotional-Intelligence-Matter-More-Than/dp/055338371X

The Center for Creative Leadership: https://www.ccl.org/

Creating a Psychologically Safe Workplace: https://hbr.org/2023/02/what-is-psychological-safety

Emotional Intelligence 2.0 by Travis Bradberry and Jean Greaves

American Psychological Association: https://www.apa.org/monitor/2018/

Weakness vs Vulnerability - What's the difference? (2023, November 23). WikiDiff. https://wikidiff.com/weakness/vulnerability

Ms, M. T. (2012, August 29). 3 Myths about Vulnerability. Psych Central. https://psychcentral.com/blog/3-myths-about-vulnerability#1

Waling, A. (2018). Rethinking Masculinity Studies: feminism, masculinity, and Poststructural Accounts of Agency and

Emotional Reflexivity. The Journal of Men's Studies, 27(1), 89–107. https://doi.org/10.1177/1060826518782980

Jharrelson. (2023, July 13). Exploring traditional masculinity definitions and societal impacts - Unmasking Masculinity. Unmasking Masculinity. https://unmasking-masculinity.com/blog/exploring-traditional-masculinity-definitions-and-societal-impacts

Men: A different Depression. (2005, July 14). https://www.apa.org. https://www.apa.org/topics/men-boys/depression

GGI Insights. (2024, February 22). Gender Roles: Navigating the Dynamics of Societal Expectations. Gray Group International. https://www.graygroupintl.com/blog/gender-roles

Pittenger, C., & Duman, R. S. (2007). Stress, Depression, and neuroplasticity: a convergence of mechanisms. Neuropsychopharmacology, 33(1), 88–109. https://doi.org/10.1038/sj.npp.1301574

Kulsum, Z. A., & Sinha, A. (2023). Gender Stereotypes, Societal Pressure and Emotional Expression among Men. ResearchGate. https://doi.org/10.25215/1103.194

Gould, W. R. (2023, March 7). Why vulnerability in relationships is so important. Verywell Mind. https://www.verywellmind.com/why-vulnerability-in-relationships-is-so-important-5193728

Vulnerability: Definition & Tips. (n.d.). The Berkeley Well-Being Institute. https://www.berkeleywellbeing.com/vulnerability.html

Romero, L. E. (2023, September 12). The power of vulnerability in leadership: experts say authenticity and honesty can move people and achieve results. Forbes. https://www.forbes.com/sites/luisromero/2023/03/08/the-power-of-vulnerability-in-leadership-experts-say-authenticity-and-honesty-can-move-people-and-achieve-results/?sh=3c39f9645ef7

Psychreg, & Psychreg. (2023, November 21). Understanding your emotions is the first step to emotional wellness. Psychreg. https://www.psychreg.org/understanding-your-emotions-first-step-emotional-wellness/

KaraMcD. (2022, April 11). 8 Benefits of Being Vulnerable that will Improve your Life. https://myquestionlife.com/benefits-of-being-vulnerable/#:~:text=8%20Benefits%20of%20Being%20Vulnerable%20that%20Will%20Drastically,8%208.%20Opens%20us%20up%20for%20growth%20

Happimynd | Read blog. (n.d.). HappiMynd. https://happimynd.com/blog/masculinity-and-mental-health-breaking-down-societal-expectations#:~:text=Societal%20expectations%20of%20masculinity%20often%20dictate%20that%20men,leading%20to%20increased%20stress%2C%20anxiety%2C%20and%20even%20depression.

Moore, M. (2022, October 11). The good kind of vulnerability. Psych Central. https://psychcentral.com/relationships/the-good-kind-of-vulnerability

Leo. (2023, October 19). What is Trust in Relationship? Exploring the Key Elements of Building Strong Bonds - Psychologily. Psychologily. https://psychologily.com/what-is-trust-in-relationship/#:~:text=Trust%20is%20the%20foundation%20of%20a%20healthy%20relationship.,to%20establish%20a%20strong%20bond%20with%20our%20partner.

Creating love in the lab: The 36 questions that spark intimacy. (2015, February 12). Berkeley. https://news.berkeley.edu/2015/02/12/love-in-the-lab/

Presence. (2022, August 23). Why the Vocabulary of Emotions is Critical to Emotional Intelligence. Presence. https://presence.com/insights/why-the-vocabulary-of-emotions-is-critical-to-emotional-intelligence/

Robinson, L. (2024, February 5). Effective communication. HelpGuide.org. https://www.helpguide.org/articles/relationships-communication/effective-communication.htm

Rcc, P. S. M. (2023b, December 11). The power of I statements: Communicating effectively. Well Beings Counselling. https://wellbeingscounselling.ca/the-power-of-i-statements/#:~:text=Key%20Takeaways%3A%201%201%20statements%20focus%20communication%20on,conflicts%2C%20providing%20feedback%2C%20and%20strengthening%20relationships.%20More%20items

American Management Association. (2023, January 26). The Five Steps to Conflict Resolution. American Management

Association. https://www.amanet.org/articles/the-five-steps-to-conflict-resolution/

MSEd, K. C. (2022, December 11). Utilizing emotional intelligence in the workplace. Verywell Mind. https://www.verywellmind.com/utilizing-emotional-intelligence-in-the-workplace-4164713

Ferebee, A. (2023, April 5). Battle of Emotions: Why men fight for feelings and what they can do to open up - Knowledge for men. Knowledge for Men. https://www.knowledgeformen.com/why-men-fight-for-feelings/

Carli, L. L. (2001). Gender and social influence. Journal of Social Issues, 57(4), 725–741. https://doi.org/10.1111/0022-4537.00238

Dovbysh, A. (2024, January 6). The art of emotional intelligence: 12 strategies for mastering your emotions. Ideapod. https://ideapod.com/the-art-of-emotional-intelligence-12-strategies-for-mastering-your-emotions/

Emotional intelligence in Leadership: Why it's important. (2019, April 3). Business Insights Blog. https://online.hbs.edu/blog/post/emotional-intelligence-in-leadership

Panchal, R. (2024, March 5). What is Emotional Leadership? Leading with Empathy And Compassion. Theleaderboy.com- Leadership Advice For Smart Leaders. https://theleaderboy.com/what-is-emotional-leadership/

Hcsuper. (2022, November 29). Daniel Goleman's Emotional Intelligence Theory: Explanation and Examples | Resilient

Educator. Resilient Educator. https://resilienteducator.com/classroom-resources/daniel-golemans-emotional-intelligence-theory-explained/

Thompkins, S. (2023, August 28). Emotional intelligence and leadership effectiveness: bringing out the best. CCL. https://www.ccl.org/articles/leading-effectively-articles/emotional-intelligence-and-leadership-effectiveness/

Team, C. (2023, October 15). Leadership styles. Corporate Finance Institute. https://corporatefinanceinstitute.com/resources/management/leadership-styles/

Coursera. (2024, February 19). Collaboration in the Workplace: Benefits and Strategies. Coursera. https://www.coursera.org/enterprise/articles/collaboration-in-workplace

González, C. (2023, June 19). Keys to foster a culture of open communication in the company. Team Insights. https://teaminsights.io/en/blog/news/keys-to-foster-a-culture-of-open-communication-in-the-company/

Iacoviello, V., Valsecchi, G., Berent, J., Borinca, I., & Falomir-Pichastor, J. M. (2021). Is traditional masculinity still valued? Men's perceptions of how different reference groups value traditional masculinity norms. the Journal of Men's Studies, 30(1), 7–27. https://doi.org/10.1177/10608265211018803

BetterHelp Editorial Team. (2024, February 22). Exploring effects of the APA's "Traditional masculinity" on men and boys | BetterHelp.

https://www.betterhelp.com/advice/mental-health-of-men-and-boys/why-does-the-apa-call-traditional-masculinity-harmful-to-men-and-boys/

Bjelland, J. (2023, December 13). Embracing sensitivity: The Crucial role of Self-Acceptance for Highly Sensitive people — Julie Bjelland. Julie Bjelland. https://www.juliebjelland.com/hsp-blog/embracing-sensitivity-the-crucial-role-of-self-acceptance-for-highly-sensitive-people

Borelli, J. L., Smiley, P. A., Gaskin, G. E., Pham, P. T., Kussman, M., & Shahar, B. (2019). Children's and Parents' Perceptions of Vulnerability as Weakness: Associations with Children's Well-Being. Journal of Child and Family Studies, 28(10), 2727–2741. https://doi.org/10.1007/s10826-019-01453-1

References (Book 1)

Field, B. (2023). Self-Sabotaging: Why does it happen. Verywell Mind. https://www.verywellmind.com/why-people-self-sabotage-and-how-to-stop-it-5207635

MindTools | Home. (n.d.). https://www.mindtools.com/ano9391/self-sabotage

Raypole, C. (2021, October 22). How Self-Sabotage holds you back. Healthline. https://www.healthline.com/health/self-sabotage

Recognizing and Overcoming Self-Sabotage | You got this! (n.d.). https://yougotthis.io/library/overcoming-self-sabotage/

Gooden, A. (2023). 6 Ways to stop negative self-talk and overcome Self doubt. Legendary Insider. https://legendaryinsider.com/6-ways-to-stop-negative-self-talk-and-overcome-self-doubt/#:~:text=Negative%20self-talk%20is%20related%20to%20self-limiting%20messages%20and,pessimism%2C%20bad%20choice-making%2C%20negative%20worldview%2C%20depression%2C%20and%20anxiety.

Scott, E., PhD. (2022). The toxic effects of negative Self-Talk. Verywell Mind. https://www.verywellmind.com/negative-self-talk-and-how-it-affects-us-4161304

Psychreg. (2021). Self-Sabotage: Coming Up with the Best Excuse to Remain in Your Comfort Zone. Psychreg. https://www.psychreg.org/self-sabotage/

Abbi. (2023, August 28). Is it time to leave your comfort zone? How leaving can spark positive change https://summer.harvard.edu/blog/leaving-your-comfort-zone/

MSEd, K. C. (2023). What is the fear of success? Verywell Mind. https://www.verywellmind.com/what-is-the-fear-of-success-5179184

Lewis, P. (2020, January 30). Why Embracing Failure Is A Big Challenge—And How To Do It Well. Forbes. https://www.forbes.com/sites/phillewis1/2020/01/30/why-embracing-failure-is-a-big-challengeand-how-to-do-it-well/?sh=615a264743e8

Drillinger, M. (2019, October 18). 7 Steps to Breaking the 'Perfectionism, Procrastination, Paralysis' Cycle Healthline. https://www.healthline.com/health/anxiety/7-steps-to-breaking-the-perfectionism-procrastination-paralysis-cycle

MSEd, K. C. (2023b). The components of attitude. Verywell Mind. https://www.verywellmind.com/attitudes-how-they-form-change-shape-behavior-2795897

Wharton Magazine. (2020, November 11). The Impact of Limiting Beliefs - Wharton Magazine. https://magazine.wharton.upenn.edu/digital/the-impact-of-limiting-beliefs/

Gowri-Kriszyk, S. (2020). Complex trauma, attachment, and Self-sabotage Stepping Stones Psychology. https://steppingstonespsychology.com/blog-resources/complex-trauma-attachment-and-self-sabotage/#:~:text=Growing%20up%20in%20an%20environment%20of%20fear%2C%20chaos%2C,i%20life%2C%20or%20that%20they%20cannot%20trust%20anyone.

Nani, M. (2023). Understanding External Validation Psychology: Why We Seek Approval from Others - Rich Woman Magazine. Rich Woman Magazine. https://richwoman.co/do-you-feel-good-enough-the-science-behind-external-validation/#:~:text=Seeking%20external%20validation%20means%20that%20we%20are%20relying,never%20enough%20to%20truly%20fill%20the%20void%20inside.

Outreach. (2022, July 29). Breaking the cycle: negative thought patterns and depression. Sage Neuroscience Center. https://sageclinic.org/blog/negative-thoughts-depression/

MSEd, K. C. (2023b). What is Self-Awareness? Verywell Mind. https://www.verywellmind.com/what-is-self-awareness-2795023

Ackerman, C. E., MA. (2023). Cognitive restructuring techniques for reframing thoughts. PositivePsychology.com. https://positivepsychology.com/cbt-cognitive-restructuring-cognitive-distortions/

Morin, A. (2023). Growth mindset: How to develop a growth mindset.. https://www.understood.org/en/articles/growth-mindset

Elizabeth. (2020). The Power of Visualization: How affirmations and visualizations work. Women's Money. https://womensmoney.com/blog/the-power-of-visualization/

MindTools | Home. (n.d.-b). https://www.mindtools.com/asjk493/the-power-of-good-habits

Roman, J. (2021, November 29). What Is the Habit Loop? — Dr. Jud. Dr. Jud. https://drjud.com/what-is-the-habit-loop/

Clear, J. (2018b, October 29). Keystone Habits: the simple way to improve all aspects of your life. James Clear. https://jamesclear.com/keystone-habits

Clear, J. (2020, February 4). How to Build New Habits: This is Your Strategy Guide. James Clear. https://jamesclear.com/habit-guide

Overcoming the pitfalls of strategy execution. (2023, July 12).https://www.strategicoffsites.com/short-pieces/overcoming-the-pitfalls-of-strategy-execution/

Learn how you can succeed at your health goals. (2023, May 9). Centers for Disease Control and Prevention. https://www.cdc.gov/diabetes/library/features/3-Steps-Building-Healthy-Habit.html

Mba, C. M. P. (2023). How to Practice Self-Compassion: 8 Techniques and tips. PositivePsychology.com. https://positivepsychology.com/how-to-practice-self-compassion/

MSEd, K. C. (2023d, May 3). How Resilience Helps You Cope With Life's Challenges. Verywell Mind. https://www.verywellmind.com/what-is-resilience-2795059

Nucleus_AI. (2023). Deep roots, tall stands: How life's challenges make us resilient. YourStory.com. https://yourstory.com/2023/07/rising-strong-navigating-lifes-storms

Cpt, S. C. (2022, September 7). The benefits of Self-Compassion. Psych Central. https://psychcentral.com/blog/practicing-self-compassion-when-you-have-a-mental-illness#1.-Self-soothing

Admin, & Admin. (2023, August 19). Embracing failure as a stepping stone to success | Bigger, badder, and better! Bigger, Badder, and Better! | Promoting strength of body, mind, and spirit. https://biggerbadderandbetter.com/embracing-failure-as-a-stepping-stone-to-success/

Nutrition, I. (2022). How to create a strong support System: 10 tips. Institute for Integrative Nutrition. https://www.integrativenutrition.com/blog/creating-a-strong-support-system

Cole, B. M. (2019, March 20). 10 Reasons Why Networking Is Essential For Your Career. Forbes. https://www.forbes.com/sites/biancamillercole/2019/03/20/why-networking-should-be-at-the-core-of-your-career/?sh=44b50b8e1300

Holland, J. (2023). Generating meaningful connections: nurturing relationships that matter. Johnny Holland. https://johnnyholland.org/2023/09/generating-meaningful-connections-nurturing-relationships-that-matter/

Weber, J. (2019, September 27). The Roles Of Allies, Mentors And Sponsors In Employee Development. Forbes. https://www.forbes.com/sites/forbeshumanresourcescouncil/2019/09/27/the-roles-of-allies-mentors-and-sponsors-in-employee-development/?sh=72e8daae38ee

Give back to experience the gift of living by contributing with Tony Robbins. (2023, June 2). tonyrobbins.com. https://www.tonyrobbins.com/giving-back/

IPC. (2023). Embracing the positive: unlocking your full potential. IPC. https://theinternationalpsychologyclinic.com/embracing-the-positive-unlocking-your-full-potential/

Todd, B. (2023, May 24). How to identify your personal strengths - 80,000 Hours. 80,000 Hours. https://80000hours.org/articles/personal-strengths/

Nair, M. (2023). 10 ways how to overcome challenges life throws at you. University of the People. https://www.uopeople.edu/blog/10-ways-how-to-overcome-challenges/

BA, C. L. (2019). What a fulfilling life actually means & 10 Secrets to Living it. Life Advancer. https://www.lifeadvancer.com/fulfilling-life/

MSEd, K. C. (2022). How to Improve Your Communication In Relationships. Verywell Mind. https://www.verywellmind.com/communication-in-relationships-why-it-matters-and-how-to-improve-5218269

The dynamics of the communication. (n.d.). http://www.benchmarkinstitute.org/t_by_t/communication/dynamics.htm

McKay, D. R. (2019). How to build and maintain a professional network. The Balance. https://www.thebalancemoney.com/building-growing-and-maintaining-a-professional-network-525834

Emotional intelligence in Leadership: Why it's important. (2019, April 3). Business Insights Blog. https://online.hbs.edu/blog/post/emotional-intelligence-in-leadership

MindTools | Home. (n.d.-c). https://www.mindtools.com/asbakxx/dwecks-fixed-and-growth-mindsets

Made in the USA
Coppell, TX
26 October 2024

39207857R00208